SOME CHRISTIAN CONVICTIONS

Some Christian Convictions

A PRACTICAL RESTATEMENT IN TERMS
OF PRESENT-DAY THINKING

By
HENRY SLOANE COFFIN

*Non enim omnis qui cogitat credit: sed cogitat
omnis qui credit, et credendo cogitat et
cogitando credit.*—AUGUSTINE

Essay Index Reprint Series

BOOKS FOR LIBRARIES PRESS
FREEPORT, NEW YORK

First Published 1915
Reprinted 1972

Library of Congress Cataloging in Publication Data

Coffin, Henry Sloane, 1877-1954.
  Some Christian convictions.

  (Essay index reprint series)
  Reprint of the 1915 ed.
  1. Theology, Doctrinal--Popular works--Addresses,
essays, lectures. I. Title.
BT77.C59 1972   230   79-167328
ISBN 0-8369-2763-X

PRINTED IN THE UNITED STATES OF AMERICA
BY
NEW WORLD BOOK MANUFACTURING CO., INC.
HALLANDALE, FLORIDA 33009

TO

D. P. C.

SOCIÆ REI HUMANÆ ATQUE DIVINÆ

PREFACE

Bishop Burnet, in his *History of His Own Time,* writes of Sir Harry Vane, that he belonged "to the sect called 'Seekers,' as being satisfied with no form of opinion yet extant, but waiting for future discoveries." The sect of Sir Harry Vane is extraordinarily numerous in our day; and at various times I have been asked to address groups of its adherents, both among college students and among thoughtful persons outside university circles, upon the fundamental beliefs of Christianity. Some of my listeners had been trained in the Church, but had thrown off their allegiance to it; others had been reared in Judaism or in agnosticism; others considered themselves "honorary members" of various religious communions—interested and sympathetic, but uncommitted and irresponsible; more were would-be Christians somewhat restive intellectually under the usual statements of Christian truths. It was for minds of this type that the following lectures were prepared. They are not an attempt at a systematic exposition of Christian doctrine, but an effort to restate a few essential Christian convictions in terms that are intelligible and persuasive to persons who have felt the force of the various intellectual movements of recent years. They do not pretend to make any contribution to scholarship; they aim at the less difficult, but perhaps scarcely less necessary middleman's task of bringing the results of the study of scholars to men and women who (to borrow a phrase of Augustine's) "believe in thinking" and wish to "think in believing."

They may be criticised by those who, satisfied with the more traditional ways of stating the historic Christian faith, will dislike their discrimination between some elements in that faith as more, and others as less, certain. I would reply that they are intentionally but a partial presentation of the Gospel for a particular purpose; and further I find my position entirely covered by the words of Richard Baxter in his *Reliquiæ*: "Among Truths certain in themselves, all are not equally certain unto me; and even of the Mysteries of the Gospel, I must needs say with Mr. Richard Hooker, that whatever men pretend, the subjective

Certainty cannot go beyond the objective Evidence: for it is caused thereby as the print on the Wax is caused by that on the Seal. I am not so foolish as to pretend my certainty to be greater than it is, merely because it is a dishonour to be less certain. They that will begin all their Certainty with that of the Truth of the Scripture, as the *Principium Cognoscendi,* may meet me at the same end; but they must give me leave to undertake to prove to a Heathen or Infidel, the Being of God and the necessity of Holiness, even while he yet denieth the Truth of Scripture, and in order to his believing it to be true."

In preparing the lectures for publication I have allowed the spoken style in which they were written to remain; several of the chapters, however, have been somewhat enlarged.

I am indebted to two of my colleagues, Professor James E. Frame and Professor A. C. McGiffert, for valuable suggestions in two of the chapters, and especially to my friend, the Rev. W. Russell Bowie, D.D., of St. Paul's Church, Richmond, Va., who kindly read over the manuscript.

CONTENTS

SOME CHRISTIAN CONVICTIONS

INTRODUCTION

Some Movements of Thought in the Nineteenth Century Which Have Affected Christian Beliefs

When King Solomon's Temple was a-building, we are told that the stone was made ready at the quarry, "and there was neither hammer nor axe nor any tool of iron heard in the house." The structures of intellectual beliefs which Christians have reared in the various centuries to house their religious faith have been built, for the most part, out of materials they found already prepared by other movements of the human mind. It has been so in our own day, and a brief glance at some of the quarries and the blocks they have yielded may help us to understand the construction of the forms of Christian convictions as they appear in many minds. Some of the quarries named have been worked for more than a century; but they were rich to begin with, and they have not yet been exhausted. Some will not seem distinctive veins of rock, but new openings into the old bed. Many blocks in their present form cannot be certainly assigned to a specific quarry; they no longer bear an identifying mark. Nor can we hope to mention more than a very few of the principal sources whence the materials have been taken. The plan of the temple and the arrangement of the stones are the work of the Spirit of the Christian Faith, which always erects a dwelling of its own out of the thought of each age.

Romanticism has been one rich source of material. This literary movement that swept over Germany, Britain, France and Scandinavia at the opening of the Nineteenth Century, itself influenced to some degree by the religious revival of the German Pietists and the English Evangelicals, was a release of the emotions, and gave a completer expression to all the elements in human nature. It brought a new feeling towards nature as alive with a spiritual Presence—

> Something far more deeply interfused
> Whose dwelling is the light of setting suns,

And the round ocean, and the living air,
And the blue sky, and in the mind of man:
A motion and a spirit, that impels
All thinking things, all objects of all thought,
And rolls through all things.

It baptized men into a new sense of wonder; everything became for them miraculous, instinct with God. It quickened the imagination, and sent writers, like Sir Walter Scott, to make the past live again on the pages of historical novels. Sights and sounds became symbols of an inner Reality: nature was to Emerson "an everlasting hint"; and to Carlyle, who never tires of repeating that "the Highest cannot be spoken in words," all visible things were emblems, the universe and man symbols of the ineffable God.

To the output of this quarry we may attribute the following elements in the structure of our present Christian thought:

(1) That religion is something more and deeper than belief and conduct, that it is an experience of man's whole nature, and consists largely in feelings and intuitions which we can but imperfectly rationalize and express. George Eliot's Adam Bede is a typical instance of this movement, when he

says: "I look at it as if the doctrines was like finding names for your feelings."

(2) That God is immanent in His world, so that He works as truly "from within" as "from above." He is not external to nature and man, but penetrates and inspires them. While an earlier theology thought of Him as breaking into the course of nature at rare intervals in miracles, to us He is active in everything that occurs; and the feeding of the five thousand with five loaves and two fishes, while it may be more startling, is not more divine than the process of feeding them with bread and fish produced and caught in the usual way. Men used to speak of Deity and humanity as two distinct and different things that were joined in Jesus Christ; no man is to us without "the inspiration of the Almighty," and Christ is not so much God *and* man, as God *in* man.

(3) That the Divine is represented to us by symbols that speak to more parts of our nature than to the intellect alone. Horace Bushnell entitled an essay that still repays careful reading, *The Gospel a Gift to the Imagination.* One of our chief complaints with the historic creeds and confessions is

that they have turned the poetry (in which religious experience most naturally expresses itself) into prose, rhetoric into logic, and have lost much of its content in the process. Jesus is to the mind with a sense for the Divine the great symbol or sacrament of the Invisible God; but to treat His divinity as a formula of logic, and attempt to demonstrate it, as one might a proposition in geometry, is to lose that which divinity is to those who have experienced contact with the living God through Jesus.

A second quarry, which Christianity itself did much to open, and from which later it brought supplies to rebuild its own temple of thought, is *Humanitarianism*. Beginning in the Eighteenth Century with its struggle for the rights of man, this movement has gone on to our own day, setting free the slaves, reforming our prisons, protesting against war and cruelty, protecting women and children from economic exploitation, and devoting itself to all that renders human beings healthier and happier.

It found itself at odds with current theological opinions at a number of points. Preachers of religion were emphasizing the total depravity of man; and humanitarians brought to the fore the humanity of Jesus, and bade them see the possibilities of every man in Christ. They were teaching the endless torment of the impenitent wicked in hell; and with its new conceptions of the proper treatment of criminals by human justice, it inveighed against so barbarous a view of God. They proclaimed an interpretation of Calvary that made Christ's death the expiation of man's sin and the reconciliation of an offended Deity; in McLeod Campbell in Scotland and Horace Bushnell in New England, the Atonement was restated, in forms that did not revolt men's consciences, as the vicarious penitence of the one sensitive Conscience which creates a new moral world, or as the unveiling of the suffering heart of God, who bears His children's sins, as Jesus bore His brethren's transgressions on the cross. They were insisting that the Bible was throughout the Word of God, and that the commands to slaughter Israel's enemies attributed to Him, and the prayers for vengeance uttered by vindictive psalmists, were true revelations of His mind; and Humanitarianism refused

to worship in the heavens a character less
good than it was trying to produce in men
on earth. These men of sensitive conscience
did for our generation what the Greek phil-
osophers of the Fifth Century B. C. did for
theirs—they made the thought of God
moral: "God is never in any way unright-
eous—He is perfect righteousness; and he
of us who is the most righteous is most like
Him" (Plato, *Theæt.* 176c.).

From this movement of thought our chief
gains have been:

(1) A view of God as good as the best of
men; and that means a God as good as
Jesus of Nazareth. Older theologians talked
much of God's decrees; we speak oftener of
His character.

(2) The emphasis upon the humanity of
Jesus and of our ability and duty to become
like Him. Spurred by Romanticism's interest in imaginatively reconstructing history,
many *Lives of Christ* have been written; and
it is no exaggeration to say that Jesus is far
better known and understood at present
than He has been since the days of the
evangelists.

A third quarry is the *Physical Sciences*. As its blocks were taken out most Christians were convinced that they could never be employed for the temple of faith. They seemed fitted to express the creed of materialism, not of the Spirit. Science was interested in finding the beginnings of things; its greatest book during the century bore the title, *The Origin of Species;* and the lowly forms in which religion and human life itself appeared at their start seemed to degrade them. Law was found dominant everywhere; and this was felt to do away with the possibility of prayer and miracle, even of a personal God. Its investigations into nature exposed a world of plunder and prey, where, as Mill put it, all the things for which men are hanged or imprisoned are everyday performances. The scientific view of the world differed totally from that which was in the minds of devout people, and with that which was in the minds of the writers of the Bible. A large part of the last century witnessed a constant warfare between theologians and naturalists, with many attempted reconciliations. Today thinking people see that the battle was due to mistakes on both sides; that there is a scientific and a religious approach to Truth; and that strife ensues only when either attempts to block the other's path. Charles Darwin wisely said, "I do not attack Moses, and I think Moses can take care of himself." Both physicists and theologians were wrong when they thought of "nature" as something fixed, so that it is possible to state what is natural and what supernatural; "nature" is plastic, responding all the while to new stimuli, and the title of a recent book, *Creative Evolution*, indicates a changed scientific and philosophical attitude towards the world.

From this scientific movement we shall find in our present Christian convictions, with much else, these items:

(1) The conception of the unity of all life. When Goethe in a flash of insight saw the structure of the entire tree in a single leaf, and of the complete skeleton of the animal in the skull of a sheep, he gave the mind of man a new assurance of the unity that pervades the whole creation. And when scientific men asserted the universality of law, they made it forever impossible for us to divide life into separate districts—the

secular and the sacred, the natural and the supernatural. Principles discovered in man's spirit in its responses to truth, to love, to companionship, to justice, hold good of his response to God. There is a "law of the spirit of life in Christ Jesus"; and it must be ascertained and worked with. But "laws" are recognized as our labels for the discoveries we have made of God's usual methods of working, and they do not stand between us and Him, barring our personal fellowship with Him in prayer, nor between Him and His world, excluding His new and completer entrances into the world's life.

(2) The thought of development or evolution as the process by which religious ideas and institutions, like all other forms of life, live and grow in a changing world.

(3) The abandonment of the attempt to prove God's existence and attributes from what can be seen in His world. We cannot expect to find in the conclusion more than the premises contain, and "nature" as it now is can never yield a personal and moral, much less a Christian, God.

And not from nature up to nature's God,
But down from nature's God look nature through.

(4) A readjustment of our view of the Bible, which frankly recognizes that its scientific ideas are those of the ages in which its various writers lived, and cannot be authoritative for us today.

(5) A larger view of God, commensurate with the older, bigger, more complex and more orderly world the physical sciences have brought to light.

A fourth source of materials, which is but another vein of this scientific quarry, is *the historical and literary investigation of the Bible.* This has not been so recently opened as is commonly supposed, but has been worked at intervals throughout the history of the Church, and notably at the Protestant Reformation. Luther carefully reëxamined the books of the Bible, and declared that it was a matter of indifference to him whether Moses was the author of the Pentateuch, pronounced the *Books of the Chronicles* less accurate historically than the *Books of the Kings,* considered the present form of the books of *Isaiah, Jeremiah* and *Hosea* probably due to later hands, and distinguished in the New Testament "chief books" from those of less moment. Calvin, too, discussed the authorship of some of the books, and suggested Barnabas as the writer of the *Epistle to the Hebrews*. But the Nineteenth Century witnessed a very thorough application to the Scriptures of the same methods of historical and literary criticism to which all ancient documents were subjected. The result was the discovery of the composite character of many books, the rearrangement of the Biblical literature in the probable order of its writing, and the use of the documents as historical sources, not so much for the periods they profess to describe, as for those in and for which they were written.

We can assign the following elements in our contemporary Christian thought to these scholarly investigations:

(1) The conception of revelation as progressive—a mode of thought that falls in with the idea of development or evolution.

(2) The distinction between the Bible as literature, with the history, science, ethics and theology of its age, and the religious experience of which it is the record, and in which we find the Self-disclosure of God.

(3) An historical rather than a specula-

tive Christ. We do not begin (however we may end) with a Figure in the heavens, the eternal Son of God, but with Jesus of Nazareth. This method of approaching Him reinforces the emphasis on His manhood which came from Humanitarianism. Christianity, like the fabled giant, Antæus, has always drawn fresh strength for its battles from touching its feet to the ground in the Jesus of historic fact. It was so when Francis of Assisi recovered His figure in the Thirteenth Century, and when Luther rediscovered Him in the Sixteenth. There can be little doubt but that fresh spiritual forces are to be liberated, indeed are already at work, from this new contact with the Jesus of history.

Still another opening in the scientific quarry is *Psychology*. The last century saw great advances in the investigation of the mind of man, which revolutionized educational methods, gave new tools to novelists and historians, and threw new light on every aspect of the human spirit. Psychologists turned their attention to religion, and have done much to chart out the movements of man's nature in his response to his highest inspirations. They have altered methods of Biblical education in our Sunday Schools, have shown us helpful and harmful ways of presenting religious appeals, and have given us scientific standards to test the value of the materials employed in public worship.

We may ascribe the following elements in our Christian thought to them:

(1) The normal character of the religious experience. Faith had been regarded as the product of deception or as an aberration of the human spirit; it now is established as a natural element in a fully developed personality. A psychological literary critic, Sainte Beuve, writes: "You may not cease to be a skeptic after reading Pascal; but you must cease to treat believers with contempt." William James has given us a great quantity of *Varieties of Religious Experience,* and he deals with all of them respectfully.

(2) The part played by the Will in religious experience. Man "wills to live," and in his struggle to conserve his life and the things that are dearer to him than life, he feels the need of assistance higher than any

he can find in his world. He "wills to believe," and discovers an answer to his faith in the Unseen. This is a reaffirmation of the definition, "faith is the giving substance to things hoped for, a test of things not seen." And the student of religious psychology has now vastly more material on which to work, because the last century opened up still another quarry for investigation in *Comparative Religion*. An Eighteenth Century writer usually divided all religions into true and false; today we are more likely to classify them as more and less developed. Investigators find in the varied faiths of mankind many striking resemblances in custom, worship and belief. It is not possible to draw sharp lines and declare that within one faith alone all is light, and within the rest all is darkness. Everything that grows out of man's experience of the Unseen is interesting, and no thought or practice that has seemed to satisfy the spiritual craving of any human being is without significance. Our own faith is often clarified by comparing it with that of some supposedly unrelated religion. Many a usage and conviction in ethnic cults supplies a suggestive parallel to something in our Bible. The development of theology or of ritual in some other religion throws light on similar developments in Christianity. The widespread sense of the Superhuman confirms our assurance of the reality of God. "To the philosopher," wrote Max Müller, "the existence of God may seem to rest on a syllogism; in the eyes of the historian it rests on the whole evolution of human thought." Under varied names, and with very differing success in their relations with the Unseen, men have had fellowship with the one living God. It was this unity of religion amid many religions that the Vedic seers were striving to express when they wrote, "Men call Him Indra, Mitra, Varuna, Agni; sages name variously Him who is but One."

This study of comparative religion has gained for us:

(1) A much clearer apprehension of what is distinctive in Christianity, and a much more intelligent understanding of the completeness of its answer to religious needs which were partially met by other faiths.

(2) A new attitude towards the missionary problem, so that Christians go not to

destroy but to fulfil, to recognize that in the existing religious experience of any people, however crude, God has already made some disclosure of Himself, that in the leaders and sages of their faith He has written a sort of Old Testament to which the Christian Gospel is to be added, that men may come to their full selves as children of God in Jesus Christ.

A final quarry, which promises to yield, perhaps, more that is of value to faith than any of those named, is the *Social Movement*. In the closing years of the Eighteenth Century social relations were looked on as voluntary and somewhat questionable productions of individuals, which had not existed in the original "state of nature" where all men were supposed to have been free and equal. The closing years of the Nineteenth Century found men thinking of society as an organism, and talking of "social evolution." This conception of society altered men's theories of economics, of history, of government. Nor did these newer theories remain in the classrooms of universities or the meetings of scientists; they became the platforms of great political parties, like the Socialists

in Germany and France, and the Labor
Party in Britain. Men are thinking, and
what is more *feeling,* today, in social terms;
they are revising legislation, producing
plays and novels, and organizing countless
associations in the interest of social advance.
We are still too much in the thick of the
movement to estimate its results, and we
can but tentatively appraise its contributions
to our Christian thought.

(1) It has given men a new interest in
religion. The intricacies of social problems
predispose men to value an invisible Ally,
and such prepossession is, as Herbert Spen-
cer said, "nine-points of belief." The social
character of the Christian religion, with its
Father-God and its ideals of the Kingdom,
gives it a peculiar charm to those whose
hearts have been touched with a passion for
social righteousness. A recent historian of
the thought of the last century, after review-
ing its scientific and philosophic tendencies,
makes the remark that "an increasing number of thinkers of our age expect the next
step in the solution of the great problems of
life to be taken by practical religion."

(2) It has made us realize that religion is

essentially social. Men's souls are born of
the social religious consciousness; are nourished by contact with the society of believers,
in fellowship with whom they grow "a larger
soul," and find their destiny in a social religious purpose—the Kingdom of God.

(3) It has taught us that religious sus-
ceptibility is intimately connected with social
status. Spiritual movements have always
found some relatively unimpressionable
classes. In primitive Christian times "not
many well-educated, not many influential,
not many nobly born were called"; and in
our own age the two least responsive strata
in society are the topmost and the bottom-
most—those so well off that they often feel
no pressure of social obligation, and those
without the sense of social responsibility because they have nothing. It is the interest
of spiritual religion to do away with both
these strata, placing social burdens on the
former and imposing social privileges on the
latter, for responsibility proves to be the
chief sacrament of religion.

(4) It has brought the Church to a new
place of prominence in Christian thought.
Men realize their indebtedness for their own

spiritual life to the collective religious experience of the past, represented in the Church; their need of its fellowship for their growth in faith and usefulness; and the necessity of organized religious effort, if society is to be leavened with the Spirit of Christ. Church membership becomes a duty for every socially minded Christian. And the social purpose renders Church unity a pressing task for the existing Christian communions. John Bunyan's pilgrim could make his progress from the City of Destruction to the New Jerusalem with a few like-minded companions; but a Christian whose aim is the transformation of the City of Destruction into the City of God needs the coöperation of every fellow believer. Denominational exclusiveness becomes intolerable to the Christian who finds a whole world's redemption laid on his conscience.

(5) It demands a social reinterpretation of many of the Church's doctrines, a reinterpretation which gives them richer meaning. The vicarious atonement of Jesus Christ, for example, becomes intelligible and kindling to those who have a social conscience and know something of bearing the guilt of

others; and the New Testament teaching of the Holy Spirit is much more real and clear to those who have felt the social spirit of our day lifting them out of themselves into the life of the community, quickening their consciences and sympathies, and giving them a sense of brotherhood with men and women very unlike themselves. Vinet wrote a generation ago, *"L'Esprit Saint c'est Dieu social."*

We have by no means exhausted the list of quarries from which stones, and stones already prepared for our purpose, can be and are taken for the edifice of our Christian convictions. The life of men with Christ in God preserves its continuity through the ages; it has to interpret itself to every generation in new forms of thought. Under old monarchies it was the custom on the accession of a sovereign to call in the coins of his predecessor and remint them with the new king's effigy. The silver and the gold remain, but the impress on them is different. The reminting of our Christian convictions is a somewhat similar process: the precious ore of the religious experience continues, but it bears the stamp of the current ruling ideas in men's view of the world. But lifeless metal, however valuable, cannot offer a parallel to the vital experiences of the human spirit. The remolding of the forms of its convictions does more than conserve the same quantity of experience; a more commodious temple of thought enables the Spirit of faith to expand the souls of men within. In theology by altering boundaries we often gain territory. We not only make the map of our soul's life with God clearer to ourselves, so that we live within its confines more intelligently; we actually increase the size of the map, and possess a larger life with God.

CHAPTER I

RELIGION

Religion is experience. It is the response of man's nature to his highest inspirations. It is his intercourse with Being above himself and his world.

Religion is *normal* experience. Its enemies call it "an indelible superstition," and its friends assert that man is born believing. That a few persons, here and there, appear to lack the sense for the Invisible no more argues against its naturalness than that occasionally a man is found to be color-blind or without an ear for music. Mr. Lecky has written, "That religious instincts are as truly part of our natures as are our appetites and our nerves is a fact which all history establishes, and which forms one of the strongest proofs of the reality of that unseen world to which the soul of man continually tends."

Some have sought to discredit religion as a surviving childishness. A baby is dependent upon its parents; and babyish spirits, they say, never outgrow this sense of dependence, but transfer that on which they rely from the seen to the unseen. While, however, other childish things, like ghosts and fairies, can be put away, man seems to be "incurably religious," and the most completely devout natures, although childlike in their attitude towards God, give no impression of immaturity. When one compares Jesus of Nazareth with the leaders in State and Church in the Jerusalem of His day, He seems the adult and they the children. And further, those who attempt to destroy religion as an irrational survival address themselves to the task of a Sisyphus. Although apparently successful today, their work will have to be done over again tomorrow. On no other battlefield is it necessary so many times to slay the slain. Again and again religion has been pronounced obsolete, but passing through the midst of its detractors it serenely goes its way. When men laboriously erect its sepulchre, faith,

Like a child from the womb, like a ghost from the tomb,
Will arise and unbuild it again.

Its indestructible vitality is evidence that it is an inherent element in human nature, that the unbeliever is a subnormal man.

Religion is an affair of the *whole* personality. Some have emphasized the part feeling plays in it. Pascal describes faith as "God felt by the heart," and Schleiermacher finds the essence of religion in the sense of utter dependence. Many of us recognize ourselves as most consciously religious in

> that serene and blessed mood
> In which the affections gently lead us on.

Our highest inspirations commonly come to us in a wistful yearning to be like the Most High, in a sense of reconciliation with Him, in a glowing enthusiasm for His cause, in the calm assurance of His guidance and protection, in the enlargement of our natures as they become aware of His indwelling. "We *feel* that we are greater than we *know*."

Others give prominence to the rôle of the intellect. God is the most reasonable explanation of the facts of life. Religious truths and men's minds harmonize as though they had been made for each other. The thought of Deity gives them perfect mental satisfaction. Dante tells us: "The life of my heart, that of my inward self, was wont to be a sweet thought which went many times to the feet of God, that is to say in thought I contemplated the kingdom of the Blessed." And a present-day English thinker, Mr. F. H. Bradley, writes: "All of us, I presume, more or less are led beyond the region of ordinary facts. Some in one way and some in another, we seem to touch and have communion with what is beyond the visible world. In various manners we find something higher which both supports and humbles, both chastens and transports us. And, with various persons, the intellectual effort to understand the universe is a principal way of their experiencing the Deity."

Still others lay the chief stress upon the will. Man wills to live; but in a universe like ours where he is pitted against overwhelming forces, he is driven to seek allies, and in his quest for them he wills to believe in a God as good as the best in himself and better. Faith is an adventure; Clement of Alexandria called it "an enterprise of noble daring to take our way to God." We trust that the Supreme Power in the world is akin to the highest within us, to the highest we discover anywhere, and will be our confederate in enabling us to achieve that highest. Kant found religion through response to the imperative voice of conscience, in "the recognition of our duties as divine commands." Pasteur, in the address which he delivered on taking his seat in the Académie Française, declared: "Blessed is he who carries within himself a God, an ideal, and who obeys it; ideal of art, ideal of science, ideal of the gospel virtues, therein lie the springs of great thoughts and great actions; they all reflect light from the Infinite."

But while all these views are correct in their affirmations, it is perilous to exalt one element in religious experience lest we slight others of equal moment. There is danger in being fractionally religious. No man really finds God until he seeks Him with his whole nature. Some persons are sentimentally believers and mentally skeptics; they stand at the door of the sanctuary with their hearts in and their heads out. Writing as an old man, Coleridge said of his youth, "My head was with Spinoza, though my whole heart remained with Paul and John."

An unreasoning faith is sure to end in folly; it is a mind all fire without fuel. A true religious experience, like a coral island, requires both warmth and light in which to rise. An unintelligent belief is in constant danger of being shattered. Hardy, in sketching the character of Alec D'Uberville, explains the eclipse of his faith by saying, "Reason had had nothing to do with his conversion, and the drop of logic that Tess had let fall into the sea of his enthusiasm served to chill its effervescence to stagnation."

Others, at the opposite extreme, are merely convinced without being converted. They are appealed to by the idea of God, rather than led into actual fellowship of life with Him. A striking instance is the historian, Edward Gibbon, who, at the age of sixteen, unaided by the arguments of a priest and without the æsthetic enticements of the Mass, was brought by his reading to embrace Roman Catholicism, and had himself baptized by a Jesuit father in June, 1753. By Christmas of 1754 he had as thoughtfully read himself out of all sympathy with Rome. He was undoubtedly sincere throughout, but his belief and subse-

quent unbelief were purely matters of
judgment. The bases of our faith lie
deeper than our intelligence. We reach
God by a passionate compulsion. We seek
Him with our reason only because we have
already been found of Him in our intuitions.

Still others use their brains busily in their
religion, but confine them within carefully
restricted limits. Outside these their faith
is an unreasoning assumption. Their mental
activity spends itself on the details of doctrine, while they never try to make clear to
themselves the foundations of their faith.
They have keen eyes for theological niceties,
but wear orthodox blinders that shut out all
disturbing facts. Cardinal Newman, for
example, declared that dogma was the essential ingredient of his faith, and that religion
as a mere sentiment is a dream and a mockery. But he was so afraid of "the all-corrod-
ing, all-dissolving skepticism of the intellect
in religious inquiries" that he placed the safe-
guard of faith in "a right state of heart,"
and refused to trust his mind to think its way
through to God. Martineau justly com-
plained that "his certainties are on the sur-

face, and his uncertainties below." We are
only safe as believers when, besides keeping
the heart clean, we

> press bold to the tether's end
> Allotted to this life's intelligence.

Those, again, who insist that in religion
the willingness is all, forget that it seems no
more in our power to believe than it is to
love. We apparently "fall into" the one as
we do into the other; we do not choose to
believe, we cannot help believing. And
unless a man's mind is satisfied with the
reasonableness of faith, he cannot "make
believe." Romanes, who certainly wished
for fellowship with the Christian God as ar-
dently as any man, confessed: "Even the
simplest act of will in regard to religion—
that of prayer—has not been performed by
me for at least a quarter of a century, simply
because it has seemed so impossible to pray,
as it were, hypothetically, that much as I
have always desired to be able to pray, I
cannot will the attempt." Christianity has
ever laid stress upon its intellectual appeal.
By the manifestation of the truth its missionaries have, from Paul's day, tried to

commend themselves. We do not hear of "Evidence Societies" among non-Christian faiths. When the Emperor Julian attempted to restore the ancient paganism, he did not argue for its superior credibility, but contented himself with abusing the creed of Christians and extolling the beauty of the rituals of the religion it had supplanted. But the propaganda of the gospel of Jesus is invariably one of persuasion, convincing and confirming men's minds with its truth.

It would be as false, however, to neglect the part a man's willingness has in his faith. To believe in the Christian God demands a severe moral effort. It can never be an easy thing to rely on love as the ultimate wisdom and power in the universe. "The will to believe," if not everything, is all but everything, in predisposing us to listen to the arguments of the faith and in rendering us inflammable to its kindling emotions.

But no man can be truly religious who is not in communion with God with "as much as in him is." Somebody has finely said that it does not take much of a man to be a Christian, but it takes all there is of him. An

early African Christian, Arnobius, tells us
that we must "cling to God with all our
senses, so to speak." And Thomas Carlyle
gave us a picture of the ideal believer when
he wrote of his father that "he was religious
with the consent of his whole faculties." It
is faith's ability to engross a man's entire
self, going down to the very roots of his
being, that renders it indestructible. It can
say of those who seek to undermine it, as
Hamlet said of his enemies:

> It shall go hard,
> But I will delve one yard below their mines.

As an experience, God is a discovery
which each must make for himself. Religion comes to us as an inheritance; and at
the outset we can no more distinguish the
voice of God from the voices of men we
respect, than the boy Samuel could distinguish the voice of Jehovah from that of Eli.
But we gradually learn to "possess our possession," to respond to our own highest inspirations, whether or not they inspire others.
Pascal well says: "It is the consent of yourself to yourself and the unchanging voice

of your own reason that ought to make you believe." So far only as we repeat for ourselves the discoveries of earlier explorers of Him who is invisible have we any religion of our own. And this personal experience is the ground of our certainty; "as we have heard, so have we seen in the city of our God."

Religious experience, and even Christian experience, appears in a great variety of forms; and there is always a danger lest those who are personally familiar with one type should fail to acknowledge others as genuine. The mystics are apt to disparage the rationalists; hard-headed, conscientious saints look askance at seers of visions; and those whose new life has broken forth with the energy and volume of a geyser hardly recognize the same life when it develops like a spring-born stream from a small trickle, increased by many tributaries, into a stately river. The value of an experience is to be judged not by its form, but by its results. Fortunately for Christianity the New Testament contains a variety of types. With the first disciples the light dawns gradually; on St. Paul it bursts in a flash brighter than

noonday. The emotional heights and depths
of the seer on Patmos contrast with the
steady level disclosed in the practical temperament of the writer of the *Epistle of
James*. But underneath the diversity there
is an essential unity of experience: all conform to that which Luther (as Harnack
summarizes his position) considered the essence of Christian faith—"unwavering trust
of the heart in God who has given Himself
to us in Christ as our Father."

Religious experience has been defined as
man's *response* to God; it often appears
rather his *search* for Him. But that is
characteristic only of the beginning of the
experience. The experienced know better
than to place the emphasis on their initiative
in establishing intercourse with the Divine.
"We love, because He first loved us," they
say. The Apostle, who speaks of his readers
as those who "have come to know God,"
stops and corrects himself, "or rather *to be
known of God*." Believers discover that
God was "long beforehand" with them.
Their very search is but an answer to His
seeking; in their every movement towards
Him, they are aware of His drawing. The

verse which begins, "My soul followeth hard
after Thee," continues "Thy right hand up-
holdeth me."

Religious experience, like all other, is
limited by a man's capacity for it; and some
men seem to have very scant capacity for
God. It is not easy to establish a point of
contact between a Falstaff or a Becky Sharp
and the Father of Jesus Christ. There is
no community of interest or kinship of spirit.
"Faith is assurance of things *hoped for;"*
and where there is no craving for God, He is
likely to remain incredible. Prepossession
has almost everything to do with the com-
mencement of belief. It is only when circumstances force a man to feel that a God
would be desirable that he will risk himself
to yield to his highest inspirations, and give
God the chance to disclose Himself to him.
It is a case of nothing venture, nothing have.
Faith is always a going out whither we know
not, but in each venture we accumulate
experience and gradually come to "know
Whom we have believed." Without the ini-
tial eagerness for God which opens the door
and sends us out we remain debarred from
ever knowing. As the *Theologia Germanica*

puts it, "We are speaking of a certain Truth which it is possible to know by experience, but which ye must believe in before ye know."

The capacity for religious experience can be cultivated. Faith, like an ear for music or taste in literature, is a developable instinct. It grows by contagious contact with fellow believers; as "the sight of lovers feedeth those in love," the man of faith is nourished by fellowship with the believing Church. It is increased by familiarity with fuller and richer experiences of God; continuous study of the Bible leads men into its varied and profound communion with the Most High. It is enlarged by private and social worship; prayer and hymn and message were born in vital experiences, and they reproduce the experience. Browning, in characteristic verse, describes the effect of the service upon the worshippers in Zion Chapel Meeting:

These people have really felt, no doubt,
A something, the motion they style the Call of them;
And this is their method of bringing about,
By a mechanism of words and tones,
(So many texts in so many groans)

A sort of reviving and reproducing,
   More or less perfectly (who can tell?),
The mood itself, which strengthens by using.

An unexpressed faith dies of suffocation, while utterance intensifies experience and leads to fresh expression; religion, like Shelley's Skylark, "singing still doth soar, and soaring ever singeth." Above all, the instinct for the Unseen is developed by exercise; obedience to our heavenly visions sharpens the eyes of the heart. Charles Lamb pictures his sister and himself "with a taste for religion rather than a strong religious habit." Such people exclude themselves from the power and peace, the limitless enrichment, of conscious friendship with the living God.

Indeed it is not conceivable that a man can have really tasted fellowship with the Most High without acquiring an appetite for more of Him. The same psalmist who speaks of his soul as satisfied in God, at once goes on, "My soul followeth hard after Thee." He who does not become a confirmed seeker for God is not likely ever to have truly found Him. There is something essentially irreligious in the attitude portrayed in the biography of Horace Walpole, who, when Queen Caroline tried to induce him to read Butler's *Analogy,* told her that his religion was fixed, and that he had no desire either to change or to improve it. A believer's heart is fixed; his soul is stayed on God; but his experience is constantly expanding.

Constancy is perhaps an inaccurate word to employ of man's intercourse with the Invisible. Even in the most stedfast and unwavering this intercourse is characterized by

> tidal movements of devoutest awe
> Sinking anon to farthest ebb of doubt.

And in the world's life there are ages of faith and ages of criticism. Both assurance and questioning appear to be necessary. Professor Royce asserts that "a study of history shows that if there is anything that human thought and cultivation have to be deeply thankful for, it is an occasional, but truly great and fearless age of doubt." And in individuals it is only by facing obstinate questionings that faith is freed from folly and attains reasonableness.

Nor can religious experience, however boldly it claims to know, fail to admit that its knowledge is but in part. Our knowledge of God, like the knowledge we have of each other, is the insight born of familiarity; but no man entirely knows his brother. And as for the Lord of heaven and earth, how small a whisper do we hear of Him! Some minds are constitutionally ill-adapted for fellowship with Him because they lack what Keats calls "negative capability"—"that is, when a man is capable of being in uncertainties, mysteries, doubts, without any irritable reaching after fact and reason. Coleridge, for instance, would let go a fine isolated verisimilitude, caught from the Penetralium of mystery, from being incapable of remaining content with half-knowledge." We have to trust God with His secrets, as well as try to penetrate them as far as our minds will carry us. We have to accustom ourselves to look uncomplainingly at darkness, while we walk obediently in the light. "They see not clearliest who see all things clear."

But to many it seems all darkness, and the light is but a phantom of the credulous. How do we know that we *know,* that the inference we draw from our experience is correct, that we are in touch with a living God who is to any extent what we fancy Him to be? Our experience consists of emotions, impulses, aspirations, compunctions, resolves; we infer that we are in communion with Another—the Christian God; but may not this explanation of our experience be mistaken?

Religious experience is self-evidencing to the religious. God is as real to the believer as beauty to the lover of nature on a June morning, or to the artistic eye in the presence of a canvas by a great master. Men are no more argued into faith than into an appreciation of lovely sights and sounds; they are immediately and overwhelmingly aware of the Invisible.

> The rest may reason, and welcome; 'tis we musicians know.

Faith does not require authority; it confers it. To those who face the Sistine Madonna, in the room in the Dresden Gallery where it hangs in solitary eminence, it is not the testimony of tradition, nor of the thousands of its living admirers throughout the world,

that renders it beautiful; it makes its own
irresistible impression. There are similar
moments for the soul when some word, or
character, or event, or suggestion within
ourselves, bows us in admiration before the
incomparably Fair, in shame before the un-
approachably Holy, in acceptance before
the indisputably True, in adoration before
the supremely Loving—moments when "belief overmasters doubt, and we know that
we know." At such times the sense of personal intercourse is so vivid that the believer
cannot question that he stands face to face
with the living God.

Such moments, however, are not abiding;
and in the reaction that follows them the
mind will question whether it has not been
the victim of illusion. John Bunyan owns:
"Though God has visited my soul with never
so blessed a discovery of Himself, yet after-
wards I have been in my spirit so filled with
darkness, that I could not so much as once
conceive what that God and that comfort
was with which I had been refreshed." Many
a Christian today knows the inspiration and
calm and reinforcement of religion, only to
find himself wondering whether these may

not come from an idea in his own head, and
not from a personal God. May we not be
in a subjective prison from whose walls
words and prayers rebound without outer
effect?

How far may we trust our experience as
validating the inferences we draw from it?
The Christian thought of God is after all no
more than an hypothesis propounded to account for the Christian life. May not our
experiences be accounted for in some other
way? We must distinguish between the
adequacy of our thought of God and the
fact that there is a God more or less like our
thought of Him. Our experience can never
guarantee the entire correctness of our con-
cept of Deity; a child experiences parental
love without knowing accurately who its
parents are—their characters, position, abil-
ities, etc. But the child's experience of
loving care convinces the child that he possesses living parents. Is it likely that, were
God a mere fancy, a fancy which we should
promptly discard if we knew it as such, our
experience could be what it is? An explanation of an experience, which would destroy
that experience, is scarcely to be received as

an explanation. Religion is incomparably
valuable, and to account for it as self-hyp-
nosis would end it for us as a piece of folly.
Can life's highest values be so dealt with?
Moreover, we cannot settle down comfort-
ably in unbelief; just when we feel most sure
that there is no God, something unsettles us,
and gives us an uncanny feeling that after
all He is, and is seeking us. We find ourselves responding, and once more we are
strengthened, encouraged, uplifted. Can a
mere imagination compass such results?

How shall we test the validity of the inference we draw from our experience?

One test is the satisfaction that it gives to
all elements in our complex personality.
One part of us may be deceived, but that
which contents the entire man is not likely
to be unreal. Arthur Hallam declared that
he liked Christianity because "it fits into all
the folds of one's nature." Further, this
satisfaction is not temporary but persistent.
In childhood, in youth, in middle age, at the
gates of death, in countless experiences, the
God we infer from our spirit's reactions to
Him meets and answers our changing needs.
Matthew Arnold writes: "Jesus Christ and

His precepts are found to hit the moral experience of mankind; to hit it in the critical
points; to hit it lastingly; and, when doubts
are thrown upon their really hitting it, then
to come out stronger than ever." Unless we
are to distrust ourselves altogether, that
which appeals to our minds as reasonable, to
our hearts as lovable, to our consciences as
commanding, and to our souls as adorable,
can hardly be "such stuff as dreams are made
on."

Nor are we looking at ourselves alone.
We are confirmed by the completer experiences of the generations who have preceded
us. "They looked unto Him and were
radiant." Those thousands of beautiful and
holy faces in each century, "lit with their
loving and aflame with God," can scarcely
have been gazing on light kindled solely by
their own imaginations.

> And all their minds transfigured so together,
> More witnesseth than fancy's images,
> And grows to something of great constancy.

Religion has written its witness into the
world's history, and we can appeal to an
eloquent past.

Look at the generations of old, and see:
Who did ever put his trust in the Lord, and was
    ashamed?
Or who did abide in His fear, and was forsaken?
Or who did call upon Him, and He despised him?

And its witness comes from today as certainly, and more widely, than from any believing yesterday. Ten thousand times ten thousand, and thousands of thousands, out of every kindred and tongue and nation, throughout the world, testify what the God and Father of Jesus Christ means to them. Are we all self-deceived?

Nor are we limited to the experiences of those who at best impress us as partially religious. For the final confirmation of our faith we look to the ideal Believer, who not only has an ampler religious experience than any other, but also possesses more power to create faith, and to take us farther into the Unseen; we look unto Jesus, the Author and Perfecter of faith. His life and death, His character and influence, remain the world's most priceless possession. Was the faith which produced them, the faith which inspired Him, an hallucination? There is contained in that life more proof that God is, than in all other approach of God to man, or of man to God.

The other test of the correctness of our inference drawn from our religious experience is its practical value, the way in which it works in life. "He that willeth to do His will shall know." Coleridge bursts out indignantly: " 'Evidences of Christianity'! I am weary of the word. Make a man feel the want of it; rouse him, if you can, to the self-knowledge of the need of it; and you may safely trust it to its own evidence." Religion approaches men saying, "O taste and see that the Lord is good." He cannot be good unless He *is*. A fancied Deity, an invention however beautiful of men's brain, supposed to be a living Being, cannot be a blessing, but, like every other falsehood, a curse. If our religion is a stained glass window we color to hide the void beyond, then in the name of things as they are, whether they have a God or not, let us smash the deceiving glass, and face the darkness or the daylight outside. "Religion is nothing unless it is true," and its workableness is the test of its truth. Behind the accepted hypotheses of science lie countless experiments; and any-

one who questions an hypothesis is simply
bidden repeat the experiment and convince
himself. Behind the fundamental conviction
of Christians are generations of believers
who have tried it and proved it. The God
and Father of Jesus is a tested hypothesis;
and he who questions must experiment, and
let God convince him. To commit one's self
to God in Christ and be redeemed from most
real sins—turned from selfishness to love,
from slavery to freedom; to trust Him in
most real difficulties and perplexities, and
find one's self empowered and enlightened;
—is to discover that faith works, and works
gloriously. A man's idea of God may be,
and cannot but be, inadequate; but it corresponds not to nothing existent, but to Someone most alive. That which comes to us
through the idea is witness of the Reality
behind it.

Nor are we confined to the witness of our
personal discoveries. There is a social attestation of the workableness of faith. The
surest way of establishing the worth of our
religious experience is to share it with
another; the strongest confirmation of the
objective existence of Him with whom we

have to do is to lead another to see Him.
The most effective defender of the faith is
the missionary. "It requires," as David
Livingstone said, "perpetual propagation to
attest its genuineness." Not they who sit
and study and discuss it, however cleverly
and learnedly, discover its truth; but they
who spend and are spent in attempting to
bring a whole world to know the redeeming
love of One who is, and who rewards with in-
dubitable sonship with Himself those who
prove wholeheartedly loyal.

For our final assurance we appeal confidently to the future. The glory of the
Lord will only be fully revealed when all
flesh see it together. But with personal certainty, based on our own experience, corrob-
orated by the testimony of all the saints, we
both wait hopefully and work tirelessly for
the day when our God through Christ shall
be all in all.

CHAPTER II

THE BIBLE

In terms of the definition of religion given in the last chapter, we may describe the Bible as the record of the progressive religious experience of Israel culminating in Jesus Christ, a record selected by the experience of the Jewish and Christian Church, and approving itself to Christian experience today as the Self-revelation of the living God.

The Bible is a *literary* record. It is not so much a book as a library, containing a great variety of literary forms—legends, laws, maxims, hymns, sermons, visions, biographies, letters, etc. Judged solely as literature its writings have never been equalled in their kind, much less surpassed. Goethe declared, "Let the world progress as much as it likes, let all branches of human research develop to their utmost, nothing will take the place of the Bible—that foundation of all culture and all education." Happily for the English-speaking world the translation

into our tongue, standardized in the King
James' Bible, is a universally acknowledged
classic; and scarcely a man of letters has
failed to bear witness to its charm and
power. While most translations lose something of the beauty and meaning of the original, there are some parts of the English
Bible which, as literature and as religion,
excel the Hebrew or Greek they attempt to
render.

The Bible is a record of *religious experience*. It has but one central figure from
Genesis to *Revelation*—God. But God is
primarily in the experience, only secondarily
in the record. All thought succeeds in
grasping but a fraction of consciousness;
thought is well symbolized in Rodin's statue,
where out of a huge block of rough stone a
small finely chiselled head emerges. With
all their skill we cannot credit the men of
faith who are behind the Bible pages with
making clear to themselves but a small part
of God's Self-disclosure to them. And when
they came to wreak thought upon expression, so clear and well-trained a mind as
Paul's cannot adequately utter what he feels
and thinks. His sentences strain and some-

times break; he ends with such expressions
as "the love of Christ which passeth knowledge," and God's "unspeakable gift."

The divine revelation which is in the experience has been at times identified with the
thought that interprets it, or even with the
words which attempt to describe it. "Faith
in the thing grows faith in the report"; and
fantastic doctrines of the verbal inerrancy
of the Bible have been held by numbers of
earnest Christians. Certain recent scholars,
acknowledging that no version of the Bible
now existing is free from error, have put
forward the theory that the original manuscripts of these books, as they came from
their authors' hands, were so completely controlled by God as to be without mistake.
Since no man can ever hope to have access
to these autographs, and would not be sure
that he had them in his hands if he actually
found them, this theory amounts to saying
with the nursery rhyme:

> Oats, peas, beans, and barley grows,
> Where you, nor I, nor nobody knows.

We have not only to collate the manuscripts
we possess and try to reconstruct the like-

liest text, but when we know what the
authors probably wrote, we must press back
of their language and ideas to the religious
experience they attempt to express.

As writers the Biblical authors do not
claim a special divine assistance. Luke, in
his preface to his gospel, merely asserts that
he has taken the pains of a careful historian,
and Paul and his various amanuenses did
their best with a language in which they
were not literary experts. The Bible reader
often has the impression that its authors'
religious experience, like Milton's sculp-
tured lion, half appears "pawing to get free
his hinder parts." Or, to change the metaphor, now one portion of their communion
with God is brought to view and now
another, as one might stand before a sea that
was illuminated from moment to moment by
flashes of lightning.

The Bible is the record of an *historic* religious experience—that of Israel which led
up to the consciousness of God in Jesus and
His followers. The investigation of the
sources of Hebrew religion has shown that
many of its beliefs came from the common
heritage of the Semitic peoples; and there

are numerous points of similarity between
Israel's faith and that of other races. This
ought not to surprise us, since its God is the
God of all men. But the more resemblances
we detect, the greater the difference appears.
The same legend in Babylonia and in Israel
has such unlike spiritual content; the identical rite among the Hebrews and among their
neighbors developed such different religious
meaning. This particular stream of religious life has a unity and a character of its
own. Its record brings into the succeeding
centuries, and still produces in our world, a
distinctive relationship with God.

The Bible is a record of *progressive* religious experience. As every poet with a new
message has to create his own public, so it
would seem that God had slowly to evolve
men who would respond to His ever higher
inspirations. When scholars arrange for us
the Biblical material in its historical order,
the advance becomes much more apparent.
Its God grows from a tribal deity to the God
of the whole world; from a localized divinity
dwelling on Sinai or at Jerusalem, as the
Greeks placed their gods on Olympus, into
the Spirit who fills heaven and earth; from

"a man of war" and a tribal lawgiver into the God whose nature is love. "By experience," said Roger Ascham, "we find out a short way by a long wandering," and it took at least ten centuries to pass from the God of Moses to the Father of Jesus Christ.

Obviously we must interpret, and at times correct, the less developed by the more perfect consciousness of God. The Scriptures, like the land in which their scenes are laid, are a land of hills and valleys, of lofty peaks of spiritual elevation and of dark ravines of human passion and doubt and cruelty; and to view it as a level plain of religious equality is to make serious mistakes. *Ecclesiastes* is by no means on the same level with *Isaiah,* nor *Proverbs* with the *Sermon on the Mount.* Doctrines and principles that are drawn from texts chosen at random from all parts of the Bible are sure to be unworthy statements of the highest fellowship with God.

Nor does mere chronological rearrangement of the material do justice to the progress; there was loss as well as gain. All mountain roads on their way to the summit go down as well as up; and their advance must be judged not from their elevation at any particular point, but from their successful approach towards their destination. The experiences of Israel reach their apex in the faith of Jesus and of His immediate followers; and they find their explanation and unity in Him. In form the Jewish Bible, unlike the Christian, has no climax; it stops, ours ends. Christians judge the progress in the religious experience of Israel by its approximation to the faith and purpose of Jesus.

The Bible is a *selected* record of religious experience. Old Testament historians often refer to other books which have not been preserved; and there were letters of St. Paul which were allowed to perish, and gospels, other than our four, which failed to gain a place in the Canon. A discriminating instinct was at work, judging between writings and writings. We know little of the details of the process by which it compiled the Old Testament. The Jewish Church spoke of its Scriptures as "the Law, the Prophets, and the Writings"; and it is probable that in this order it made collections of those books which it found expressed and

reproduced its faith. In the time of Jesus
the Old Testament, as we know it, was practically complete, although there still lingered
some discussion whether *Esther, Ecclesiastes*
and the *Song of Songs* were sacred books.
We should like to know far more than students have yet discovered of the reasons
which Jewish scholars gave for admitting
some and rejecting other writings; but,
whatever their alleged reasons, the books
underwent a struggle for recognition, and
the fittest, according to the judgment of the
corporate religious experience of the devout,
survived.

The first Christians found the Jewish
Bible in use as containing "the oracles of
God"; and as it had been their Lord's Bible
it became theirs. No one of the first generation of Christians thought of adding other
Scriptures. In that age the Coming of the
Messiah and His Kingdom in power were
daily expected, and there seemed no need of
writing anything for succeeding times.
Paul's letters were penned to meet current
needs in the churches, and were naturally
kept, reread and passed from church to
church. As the years went by and disciples

were added who had never known the Lord
in the days of His flesh, a demand arose for
collections of His sayings.   Then gospels
were written, and the New Testament literature came into existence, although no one yet
thought of these writings as Holy Scripture.

Three factors, however, combined to give
these books an authoritative position.   In
the Church services *reading* was a part of
worship.   What should be read?   A letter
of an apostle, a selection of Jesus' sayings,
a memoir of His life, an account of the earliest days of the Church.   Certain books became favorites because they were most helpful in creating and stimulating Christian
faith and life; and they won their own position of respect and authority.

Some books by reason of their *authorship*
—Paul or Peter, for instance—or because
they contained the life and teaching of Jesus,
naturally held a place of reverence.   This
eventually led to the ascription to well-
known names of books that were found helpful which had in fact been written by others.
For example, the *Epistle to the Hebrews*
was ultimately credited to Paul, and the

Second Epistle of Peter to the Apostle
Peter.

And, again, *controversies* arose in which
it was all important to agree what were the
sources to which appeal should be made.
The first collection of Christian writings, of
which we know, consisting of ten letters of
Paul and an abridged version of the *Gospel
according to Luke,* was put forth by Mar-
cion in the Second Century to defend his
interpretation of Christianity—an interpretation which the majority of Christians did
not accept. It was inevitable that a fuller
collection of writings should be made to
refute those whose faith appeared incom-
plete or incorrect.

In the last quarter of the Second Century
we find established the conception of the
Bible as consisting of two parts—the Old
and the New Covenant. This meant that
the Christian writings so acknowledged
would be given at least the same authority
as was then accorded to the Jewish Bible.
Early in the Fourth Century the historian,
Eusebius, tells us how the New Testament
stood in his day. He divides the books into
three classes—those acknowledged, those

disputed, and those rejected. In the second division he places the epistles of *James* and *Jude,* the *Second Epistle of Peter* and the *Second* and *Third* of *John;* in the first all our other books, but he says of the *Revelation of John,* that some think that it should be put in the third division; in the third he names a number of books which are of interest to us as showing what some churches regarded as worthy of a place in the New Testament, and used as they did our familiar gospels and epistles. By the end of that century, under the influence of Athanasius and the Church in Rome, the New Testament as it now stands became almost everywhere recognized.

The reason given for the acceptance or rejection of a book was its *apostolic authorship.* Only books that could claim to have been written by an apostle or an apostolic man were considered authoritative. We now know that not all the books could meet this requirement; but the Church's real reason was its own discriminating spiritual experience which approved some books and refused others. Dean Sanday sums up the selective process by saying: "In the fixing of the Canon, as in the fixing of doctrine, the decisive influence proceeded from the bishops and theologians of the period 325-450. But behind them was the practice of the greater churches; and behind that again was not only the lead of a few distinguished individuals, but the instinctive judgment of the main body of the faithful. It was really this instinct that told in the end more than any process of quasi-scientific criticism. And it was well that it should be so, because the methods of criticism are apt to be, and certainly would have been when the Canon was formed, both faulty and inadequate, whereas instinct brings into play the religious sense as a whole. Even this is not infallible; and it cannot be claimed that the Canon of the Christian Sacred Books is infallible. But experience has shown that the mistakes, so far as there have been mistakes, are unimportant; and in practice even these are rectified by the natural gravitation of the mind of man to that which it finds most nourishing and most elevating."

In their attitude towards the Canon all Christians agree that the books deemed authoritative must record the historic revela-

tion which culminated in Jesus and the
founding of the Christian Church. A
Roman Catholic may derive more religious
stimulus from the *Spiritual Exercises* of
Ignatius Loyola than from the *Book of
Lamentations,* and a Protestant from Bunyan's *Pilgrim's Progress* than from the
Second Epistle of John; but neither would
think of inserting these books in the Canon.
He who finds as much religious inspiration
in some modern poet or essayist as in a book
of the Bible, may be correctly reporting his
own experience; but he is confusing the purpose of the Bible if he suggests the substi-
tution of these later prophets for those of
ancient Israel. The Bible is the spiritually
selected record of a particular Self-disclosure of God in a national history which
reached its religious goal in Jesus Christ.

Romanists and Protestants differ as to
how many books constitute the Canon, the
former including the so-called *Apocrypha*—
books in the Greek translation but not in the
original Hebrew Bible. And they differ
more fundamentally in the principle underlying the selection of the books. The Roman
Catholic holds that it is the Church which

officially has made the Bible, while the Protestant insists that the books possess spiritual qualities of their own which gave them their place in the authoritative volume, a place which the Church merely recognized. Luther, in his celebrated dispute with Dr. Eck, asserted: "The Church cannot give more authority or force to a book than it has in itself. A Council cannot make that be Scripture which in its own nature is not Scripture." The Council of Trent, answering the Reformers, in 1546, issued an official decree defining what is Scripture: "The holy, ecumenical and general Synod of Trent, legitimately convened in the Holy Ghost . . . receives and venerates with an equal piety and reverence all the books as well of the Old as of the New Testament . . . together with the traditions pertaining both to faith and to morals, as proceeding from the mouth of Christ, or dictated by the Holy Spirit, and preserved in the Church Catholic by continuous succession." Then follows a catalogue of the books, and an anathema on all who shall not receive them "as they are contained in the old vulgate Latin version."

Over against this the Protestant takes the position that the books of the Scripture came to be recognized as authoritative exactly as Shakespeare, Milton and Wordsworth have been accorded their place in English literature. It was the inherent merit of *Hamlet* and *Paradise Lost* and the *Ode on the Intimations of Immortality* that led to their acknowledgment. No official body has made Shakespeare a classic; his works have won their own place. No company of men of letters officially organized keeps him in his eminent position; his plays keep themselves. The books of the Bible have gained their positions because they could not be barred from them; they possess power to recanonize themselves. Some are much less valuable than others, and it is, perhaps, a debatable question whether one or two of the apocryphal books—*First Maccabees,* or *Ecclesiasticus,* for instance—are not as spiritually useful as the *Song of Solomon* or *Esther;* but of the chief books we may confidentially affirm that, if one of them were dug up for the first time today, it would gradually win a commanding place in Christian thought. And it is a similar social experience of the Church—Jewish and Christian—which has recognized their worth. The modernist Tyrrell has written: "It cannot be denied that in the life of that formless Church, which underlies the hierarchic organization, God's Spirit exercises a silent but sovereign criticism, that His resistlessly effectual judgment is made known, not in the precise language of definition and decree, but in the slow manifestation of practical results; in the survival of what has proved itself life-giving; in the decay and oblivion of all whose value was but relative and temporary."

In a sense each Protestant Christian is entitled to make up a Bible of his own out of the books which record the historical discoveries of God. He is not bound by the opinions of others, however many and venerable; and unless a book commends itself to his own spiritual judgment, he is under no obligation to receive it as the word of God to him. As a matter of fact every Christian does make such a Bible of his own; the particular passages which "grip" him and reproduce their experiences in him, they, and they alone, are his Bible. Luther was quick-

ened into life by the epistles of Paul, but
spoke slightingly of *James;* many socially
active Christians in our day live in the
prophets and the first three gospels, and
almost ignore the rest of the Bible. But
individual taste, while it has preferred
authors and favorite works, does not think
of denying to Milton, or Wordsworth, or
Shelley, their place among English classics;
a social judgment has assigned them that.
A man who is not hopelessly conceited will
regret his inability to appreciate a single
one of the great authors, and will try to enlarge his sympathies. The Christian will,
with entire naturalness, be loyal to so much
of the Bible as "finds him," and humbly hope
and endeavor to be led into ampler ranges
of spiritual life, that he may "apprehend
with all saints" the breadth, length, depth
and height of the historic Self-revelation of
God.

The Bible is thus *a standard of religious
experience.* If there is any question as to
what man's life with God ought to be, it can
be referred to the life recorded in these
books. But men have often made the Bible
much more; confusing experience with its

interpretation in some particular epoch, they used the Bible as a treasury of proof texts for doctrines, or of laws for conduct, or of specific provisos for Church government and worship.   They forgot that the writers of the early chapters of *Genesis,* in describing their faith in God's relationship to His world and to man and to history, had to express that faith in terms of the existing traditions concerning the creation, the fall, the deluge, the patriarchs.   Their faith in God is one thing; the scientific and historic accuracy of the stories in which they utter it is quite another thing.   They did not distinguish between Paul's life with God in Christ, and the philosophy he had learned in Gamaliel's classroom, or picked up in the thought of the Roman world of his day.   Paul's religious life is one thing, his theology in which he tries to explain and state it is another thing. They read the plans that were made for the organization of the first churches, and hastily concluded that these were intended to govern churches in all ages.   The chief divisions of the Church claim for their form of government—papal, episcopal, presbyterian, congregational—a Biblical authority.

The religious life of the early churches is one thing; their faith and hope and love ought to abide in the Church throughout all generations; the method of their organization may have been admirable for their circumstances, but there is no reason we should consider it binding upon us in the totally different circumstances of our day. Latterly social reformers have been attempting to show that the Bible teaches some form of economic theory, like socialism or communism. It lays down fundamental principles of brotherhood, of justice, of peaceableness, but the economic or political systems in which these shall be embodied, we must discover for ourselves in each age. It is the norm of our life with God; but it is not a standard fixing our scientific views, our theological opinions, our ecclesiastical polity, our economic or political theories. It shows forth the spirit we should manifest towards God and towards one another as individuals, and families, and nations; "and where the Spirit of the Lord is, there is liberty."

This brings us to the question of the *authority* of the Bible. There are two views of its authority; one that it contains mysteries beyond our reason, which are revealed to us, and guaranteed to us as true, either by marvellous signs such as miracles and fulfilled prophecies, or by the infallible pronouncement of the official Church; the other is that the Bible is the revelation of self-evidencing truth. The test of a revelation is simply that it reveals. The evidence of daylight lies in the fact that it enables us to see, and as we live in the light we are more and more assured that we really do see. Advocates of the former position say: "If anything is in the Bible, it must not be questioned; it must simply be accepted and obeyed." Advocates of the latter view say: "If it is in the Bible, it has been tried and found valuable by a great many people; question it as searchingly as you can, and try it for yourself, and see whether it proves itself true or not."

These two views came into collision in the struggle for a larger faith which we call the Reformation. Augustine had stated the position which became traditional when he wrote, "I would not believe in the Gospel without the authority of the Church." But Luther insisted on the contrary: "Thou must not place thy decision on the Pope, or any other; thou must thyself be so skilful that thou can'st say, 'God says this, not that.' Thou must bring conscience into play, that thou may'st boldly and defiantly say, 'That is God's word; on that will I risk body and life, and a hundred thousand necks if I had them.' Therefore no one shall turn me from the word which God teaches me, and that must I know as certainly as that two and three make five, that an ell is longer than a half. That is certain, and though all the world speak to the contrary, still I know that it is not otherwise. Who decides me there? No man, but only *the Truth* which is so perfectly certain that nobody can deny it." And Calvin took the same ground: "As to their question, How are we to know that the Scriptures came from God, if we cannot refer to the decree of the Church, we might as well ask, How are we to distinguish light from darkness, white from black, bitter from sweet."

The truth of the religious experiences recorded in the Bible is self-evidencing to him who shares these experiences, and to no one else. The Bible has, in a sense, to create or evoke the capacities by which it is appreciated and verified. It is inspired only to those who are themselves willing to be controlled by similar inspirations; it is the word of God only to those who have ears for God's voice. There is a difference between the phrases: "It is certain," and "I am certain." In other matters we appeal to the collective opinion of sane people; but such knowledge does not suffice in religion. Our fellowship with God must be our own response to our highest inspirations. The Bible is authoritative for us only in so far as we can say: "I have entered into the friendship of the God, whose earlier friendship with men it records, and know Him, who speaks as personally to my conscience through its pages, as He spake to its writers. The Spirit that ruled them, the Spirit of trust and service, controls me." This is John Calvin's position. "It is acting a preposterous part," he writes in his *Institutes,* "to endeavor to produce sound faith in the Scriptures by disputations. Religion appearing to profane men to consist wholly in opinion, in order that they may not believe anything on foolish or slight grounds, they wish and expect it to be proved that Moses and the prophets spake by divine inspiration; but as God alone is a sufficient witness of Himself in His own word, so also the word will never gain credit in the hearts of men, till it is confirmed by the testimony of the Spirit."

If, then, the authority of the Bible depends upon the witness of the Spirit within our own souls, its authority has definite limits. We can verify spiritually the truth of a religious experience by repeating that experience; but we cannot verify spiritually the correctness of the report of some alleged event, or the accuracy of some opinion. We can bear witness to the truthfulness of the record of the consciousness of shame and separation from God in the story of the fall of Adam and Eve; we must leave the question of the historicity of the narrative and the scientific view of the origin of the race in a single pair to the investigations of scholars. Our own knowledge of Jesus Christ as a living Factor in our careers confirms the experience His disciples had of His continued intercourse with them subsequent to His crucifixion; but the manner of His resurrection and the mode in which *post mortem* He communicated with them must be left to the untrammelled study of historical students. The religious message of a miraculous happening, like the story of Jonah or of the raising of Lazarus, we can test and prove: disobedience brings disaster, repentance leads to restoration; faith in Christ gives Him the chance to be to us the resurrection and the life. The reported events must be tested by the judgments of historic probability which are applied to all similar narratives, past or present. The Bible's authority is strictly *religious;* it has to do solely with God and man's life with man in Him; and, when read in the light of its culmination in Christ, it approves itself to the Spirit of Christ within Christians as a correct record of their experiences of God, and the mighty inspiration to such experiences. Surely it is no belittling limitation to say of this unique book that it is an authority *only on God.* Every fundamental question of life is answered, every essential need of the soul is met, when God is found, and becomes our Life, our Home.

And with such *self-evidencing* authority

in the books of the Bible, it is a question of minor importance who were their authors and when they were written—the questions which the literary historical criticism undertakes to answer. Luther put the matter conclusively when he said in his vigorous fashion: "That which does not teach Christ is not apostolic, though Peter or Paul should have said it; on the contrary that which preaches Christ is apostolic, even if it should come from Judas, Annas, Pilate and Herod." Some persons have been greatly troubled in the last generation by being told that scholars did not consider the conventionally received authorships of many of the books of the Bible correct, but thought that Moses did not write the Pentateuch, or David the *Psalms,* or Solomon the *Proverbs* or *Ecclesiastes,* or Isaiah and Jeremiah more than parts of the books that bear their names, or John and Peter all the writings ascribed to them. We are not to judge of writings by their authors, but by their intrinsic value. Suppose Shakespeare did not write more than a fraction of the plays associated with his name, or that he wrote none of them at all; the plays themselves remain as valuable as ever; their interpretation of life in its tragedy and humor, its heights and its depths, is as true as it ever was. Whatever views of their composition or authorship may be reached by literary experts, the Scriptures possess exactly the same spiritual power they have always possessed. "Lord, Thou has been our dwelling-place in all generations," whether Moses or some other psalmist penned that line; and Jesus is the bread of life, whether the apostle John or some other disciple whom Jesus loved records that experience. Scholars may make the meaning of the Scriptures much plainer by their searching studies; and they must be encouraged to investigate as minutely and rigorously as they can. To be fearful that the Bible cannot stand the test of the keenest study, is to lack faith in its divine vitality. To found a "Bible Defence League" is as unbelieving as to inaugurate a society for the protection of the sun. Like the sun the Bible defends itself by proving a light to the path of all who walk by it. The only defence it needs is to be used; and the only attack it dreads is to be left unread.

And in speaking of the authority of the

Bible we cannot forget that it is not for
Christians the supreme authority. "One is
your Master, even Christ." We must be
cautious in speaking of the Bible, as we
commonly do, as "the word of God." That
title belongs to Jesus. The Bible contains
the word of God; He is for us *the* Word of
God. We dare not overlook His untrammelled attitude towards the Scriptures of
His people, who let His own spiritual dis-
cernment determine whether a Scripture
was His Father's living voice to Him, or
only something said to men of old time, and
given temporarily for the hardness of hearts
that could respond to no higher ideal. As
His followers, we dare not use less freedom
ourselves. We test every Scripture by the
Spirit of Christ in us: whatever is to us un-
christlike in Joshua or in Paul, in a psalmist
or in the seer on Patmos, is not for us the
word of our God: whatever breathes the
Spirit of Jesus from *Genesis* to *Revelation*
is to us our Father's Self-revealing speech.

Nor do we think that God ceased speaking
when the Canon of the Bible was complete.
How could He, if He be the living God?
"Truth," said Milton, "is compared in Scrip-

ture to a streaming fountain; if her waters
flow not in a perpetual progression, they
sicken into a muddy pool of conformity and
tradition." The fountain of God's Self-
revealing still streams. Religious truth
comes to us from all quarters—from events
of today and contemporaneous prophets,
from living epistles at our side and the still
small voice within; but as a simple matter of
fact, its main flow is still through this book.
When we want God—want Him for our
guidance, our encouragement, our correc-
tion, our comfort, our inspiration—we find
Him in the record of these ancient experiences of His Self-unveiling. When near his
death, after years of agony on his bed, when
he himself had become a changed man, Hein-
rich Heine wrote: "I attribute my enlighten-
ment entirely and simply to the reading of
a book. Of a book? Yes! and it is an old
homely book, modest as nature—a book
which has a look modest as the sun which
warms us, as the bread which nourishes us—
a book as full of love and blessing as the old
mother who reads in it with her trembling
lips, and this book is *the* Book, the Bible.
With right is it named the Holy Scriptures.

He who has lost his God can find Him again
in this book; and he who has never known
Him, is here struck by the breath of the
Divine Word."

CHAPTER III

JESUS CHRIST

Three elements enter into every Christian's conception of his Lord—history, experience and reflection. Jesus is to him a figure out of the past, a force in the present, and a fact in his view of the universe. Whether we be discussing the Christ of Paul, or of the Nicene theologians, or of some thoughtful believer today, we must allow for the memory of the Man of Nazareth handed down from those who knew Him in the flesh, the acquaintance with the Lord of life resulting from personal loyalty to His will, and the explanation of this Lord reached by the mind, as, using the intellectual methods of its age, it tries to set His figure in its mental world.

The Jesus of the primitive Church was One whom believers worshipped as the Christ of God, in whose person and mission they saw the fulfilment of Israel's prophecy and the inauguration of a new religious era.

They represent their conception of Him as corresponding to and created by His own consciousness of Himself. He was aware of a unique relationship to God—He is His Son, *the* Son. And because of this divine sonship He is the Messiah, commissioned to usher in the Kingdom of God, and to bring forgiveness and eternal life to men. This He does by becoming their Teacher and their lowly Servant, laying down His life for them in suffering and death, and rising and returning to them as their Lord. He appeals to them for faith in God, for loyalty to Himself as God's Servant and Son, and for trust in His divine power to save them.

This conception of Jesus is given us in documents which must be investigated and appraised as sources of historical knowledge. The four gospels are our principal informants, and no other writings in existence have been so often and so minutely examined. Among scholars at present it is a common hypothesis that Mark's is the earliest narrative; that this was combined with a *Collection of Sayings* (compiled, perhaps, by Matthew) and other material in our first gospel, and by another editor (probably Luke) with the same or a similar *Collection of Sayings* and still other material in our third gospel. Later yet, a fourth evangelist interpreted for the world of his day the Jesus of the first three gospels in the light of his own and the Church's spiritual experience.

The earlier sources, as is usually and naturally the case with literary records of the past, are considered historically more reliable than the later. The words of Jesus in the form in which they are given in the Synoptists are more nearly as Jesus spoke them, than in the form in which they are recorded in *John.* There is a tendency, often found in kindred documents, to make events more marvellous as the tradition is handed on. In *Mark,* for instance, the Spirit descends upon Jesus "as a dove," symbolizing the quietness with which the Divine Power possessed Him; in *Luke,* the symbol is materialized, and the Holy Spirit descends "in *bodily form* as a dove." The writers interpret the narrative for their readers: *Matthew* takes Jesus' ideal of the indissoluble marriage-tie, as it is given in *Mark,* and allows, in the practical application of the ideal, divorce for adultery; he adds to Jesus'

word about telling one's brother his fault
"between thee and him alone" further advice
as to what shall be done if the brother be
obdurate, ending with "Tell it unto the
Church." *John* substitutes for the many
sayings of Jesus in the earlier gospels, in
which He appears to look forward to a
speedy and sudden coming of His Kingdom
in power, other sayings, in which He promises to come again spiritually and dwell in
His followers. On the other hand, in some
particulars scholars think that the later
writers had more accurate information, and
used it to correct misunderstandings con-
veyed by their predecessors; the length of
our Lord's ministry, the procedure followed
at the trial, the date of the crucifixion, are
by many supposed to be more exactly given
in *John* than in the Synoptists. In general
there is no reason for questioning the data
in the later sources, save as they seem to
come from an interest of the Church of their
day, unrelated with the Jesus of the earlier
records.

In such documents we must expect some
events to be supported by more historic
proof than others. The evidence for Jesus'

resurrection (to take a typical case), is far weightier than that for His birth of a virgin-mother. There is probably no scrap of primitive Christian literature which does not assume the risen Christ; and the origin of the Christian Church, and the character of its message and life, cannot be explained apart from the Easter faith in the Lord's victory over death and presence with His people in power. The virgin-birth rests on but two records (possibly on only one), neither of which belongs to the earlier strata of the tradition, and which are with difficulty reconciled with the more frequently mentioned fact that Jesus is the Son of David (an ancestry traced through Joseph). But in discussing the historicity of the narratives, it is just to the evangelists to recall that their main purpose was not the writing of history as such, but the presentation of material (which undoubtedly they considered trustworthy historically) designed to convey to their readers a correct religious estimate of Jesus Christ. "These are written that ye may believe that Jesus is the Christ, the Son of God; and that believing ye may have life in His name." They do not often take the

trouble to tell us on what evidence they report an event or a saying; they either did not
know, or they did not care to preserve, the
sequence of events, so that it is impossible
to make a harmony of the gospels in which
the material is chronologically arranged.
But they spare themselves no pains to give
the truth of the religious impression of Jesus
which they had received.

And when one compares all our documents, it is significant that they do not give
us discordant estimates of the religious
worth of Jesus. The meaning for faith of
the Christ of *John* is not at variance with the
meaning for faith of the Christ of *Mark,* or
of the Christ of the supposed *Collection of
Sayings.* The Church put the four gospels
side by side in its Canon, and has continued
to use them together for centuries, because
it has found in them a religiously harmonious
portrait of its Lord. This is also true of the
portraits of Jesus to be found in the *Acts*
and the epistles. The Christ of the entire
New Testament makes upon us *a consistent
religious impression;* and the unity of His
significance for faith is all the more note-
worthy because of the different forms of

thought in which the various writers picture
Him. Behind the primitive Church stands
an historic Figure who so stamped the impress of His personality upon believing
spirits, that, amid puzzling discrepancies of
historical detail and much variety of theological interpretation, a single religious
image of Him remains. We, whose aim is
not primarily to reconstruct the figure of
Jesus for purposes of scientific history, but
to arrive at an intelligent conviction of His
spiritual worth, are entirely satisfied with a
portrait which correctly represents the religious impression of the historic Jesus.

Two diametrically opposed classes of
scholars have denied that in the Christ of the
gospels we possess such a trustworthy report. A very few have held that the evangelists do not record an historic life at all,
but describe a Saviour-God who existed in
the faith of the Church of the First Century.
The allusions, however, in the letters of Paul
alone to definite historical associations connected with Jesus are sufficient to confute
this view. There undoubtedly was a Jesus
of Nazareth. Moreover, the divine redeemers of mythology, of whom this theory

makes so much, are most unlike the Jesus of
the gospels in moral character and religious
power; and the old argument is still perti-
nent that it would have required a Jesus to
have imagined the Jesus of the evangelists'
story.

A much larger number of scholars, deter-
mined beforehand by their philosophic views
to reject all elements in the records which
transcend usual human experience, have for
several generations sought to reconstruct the
figure of Jesus on an entirely naturalistic
basis. Instead of the Jesus of the gospels,
they give us, as the actual Man, Jesus the
Sage, or the Visionary, or the Prophet, or
the Philanthropist, who, they think, was
subsequently deified by His followers. Such
reconstructions handle the sources arbi-
trarily, eliminating from even the earliest of
them that which clashes with their precon-
ceptions. They fail to do justice to Jesus'
consciousness of Himself, of His unique
relation to God, of His all-important mission to men, as the critically investigated
documents disclose it. Historically, they do
not give us a Figure sufficiently significant
for faith to account for the Christian

Church; scientifically, their portraits do not long prove satisfactory, and are soon discarded on further investigation of the facts; and religiously, they do not appeal to Christian believers as adequate to explain their own life in Christ.

It is not surprising that these attempts have failed. The historic Jesus did not make the same impression upon everybody who met Him; men's judgments of Him varied with their spiritual capacities, and their spiritual capacities affected what He could do for them. There is enough historicity in the narratives to convince sober historians, whatever their faith or unfaith, that Jesus existed as a man among men, and that He was conscious of a relationship to God and a significance for men which transcend anything in ordinary human experience. It requires something more than sound historic judgment to see in Jesus what He saw in Himself, or what Peter saw in Him when he called Him "the Christ of God." We can never prove to any man on the basis of historical research alone that the portrait of Jesus in the gospels correctly represents the *religious* impression of the historic Jesus.

When we deal with anything religious, a subjective element enters and determines the conclusion, exactly as the artistic spirit alone can appreciate that which has to do with art. The gospels as appreciations appeal only to the similarly appreciative. We can show that the earliest stratum of the gospel tradition, according to the most rigorous methods of critical analysis, gives us a Jesus who possessed a meaning for His followers akin to the meaning the Jesus of our four gospels possessed for the Church of the First Century, and possesses for the Church of our day. Only as Jesus comes to have a supreme worth to any man can he believe that the estimate of their Master in the minds of the first disciples can be the accurate impression of a real man.

When, then, we speak of the Christ of history, we mean not the figure of Jesus as reproduced by scientific research apart from Christian faith, but the Christ of the four gospels, whose figure corresponds to the religious impression received from the historic Jesus by His earliest followers. *Lives of Christ* by historical students have their value when our main aim is historical information; but the best of them is poor indeed compared with our gospels when we wish to attain the life of Christ's followers. The humblest reader of the New Testament has the same chance with the most learned scholar of attaining a true knowledge of Jesus for religious purposes; and Jesus remains, as He would surely wish to remain, a democratic figure accessible to all in the simply told narratives of the evangelists.

Each age seems to have its own way of phrasing its religious needs; and various elements in the picture of Jesus have been prized by the succeeding ages as of special worth. Our generation finds itself religiously most interested in three outstanding features in the record of His life:

(1) *His singular religious experience.* His first followers were impressed with His unique relation to God when they saw in Him the awaited Messiah. The narratives represent Him as invariably trusting, loving, obeying the Most High as the Father, Lord of heaven and earth. His sayings lay special stress on God's tender personal interest in every child of His, on His stern judgment of hypocrites, on His Self-sacrificing

love, and on His kindness to the unthankful
and the evil. While it is not easy for us with
the limited materials at hand to discriminate
clearly between the elements in Jesus'
thought of God which He shared with His
contemporaries, and those which were His
own contribution, so discerning a believer
as Paul, reared in the most earnest circles of
Jewish thought, could not name the God to
whom he had been brought through Jesus,
without mentioning Jesus Himself; God
was to him "the God and Father of our
Lord Jesus Christ." The Deity Paul worshipped may be described as that loving
Response from the unseen which answered
the trust of Jesus; or rather that personal
Approach to man from the unseen which
produced Jesus. Men who had not been
atheists before they became Christians are
addressed by another writer as "through
Jesus believers in God." It is not enough
to say that in Jesus' experience God was
Father; others before Him, both within and
without Israel, had known the Divine Fatherhood. It was the fatherliness in God
which evoked and corresponded to Jesus'
sonship, that formed His new and distinctive

contribution. A mutual relationship is expressed in the saying: "No one knoweth the Son, save the Father; neither doth any know the Father, save the Son." Moving familiarly as a man among men, Jesus did not hesitate to offer them forgiveness, health, power, life; and to offer all these as His own possessions through His peculiar touch with the Most High—"All things have been delivered unto Me of My Father." In the words of the late Professor G. W. Knox, "Jesus set forth communion with God as the most certain fact of man's experience, and in simple reality made it accessible to everyone."

His consciousness of God was not something wholly new; He was not "a lonely mountain tarn unvisited by any stream," but received into His soul the great river of a nation's spiritual life. He was the heir of the faith of His people, and regarded Himself as completing that which a long line of predecessors had begun. He did not find it necessary to invent new terms to express His thought; but as He passed the old words through the alembic of His mind they came out with new meaning. His originality con-

sisted in His discriminating appropriation of
His inheritance, and in His using it so that it
became alive with new power. Madame de
Staël said that Rousseau "invented nothing,
but set everything on fire." Jesus took the
religion of Israel, and lived its life with God,
and after Him it possessed a kindling flame
it had never shown before. The faith of a
small people in a corner of the Roman Empire, with a few thousands of proselytes here
and there in the larger towns about the
Mediterranean, became in a generation a
force which entirely supplanted the Jewish
missionary movement and rapidly spread
throughout the world.

(2) *A singular character.* More striking
than anything Jesus said or did is what He
was. That which He worshipped in the God
He trusted, He Himself embodied. We
can estimate His character best, not by trying to inventory its virtues (for a very similar list might be attributed to others of far
less moral power) but by feeling the effect
He had on those who knew Him. They are
constantly telling us how He amazed them,
awed them, and bound them to Himself.
Their superlative tribute to Him is that,

holding His own pure and exalted view of God, they felt no incongruity in thinking of Him as beside God on the throne. It may have been their belief in His Messiahship, accredited by His resurrection and destining Him to come with power and judge the world, that led them to place Him at the right hand of God; but there was the place where He seemed to them to belong. None have ever conceived God more highly than they who said, "God is love," and these men set Jesus side by side with God. The evangelists do not attempt to describe what He was like; they let us hear Him and watch Him, as He lived in the memories of those who had been with Him; and He makes His own impression. The crowning tribute is that we have no loftier adjective in our vocabulary than "Christlike."

(3) *A singular victory*—a victory over the world and sin and death.

Jesus believed in and proclaimed a new order of things in the world—the Kingdom of God—in which His Father's will should be realized. It was an order in which men should live in love with one another and with God, in which justice, kindness and faithfulness should prevail in all relationships, and in which all God's children's needs should be supplied, their maladies healed, their wrongs righted, their lives made full. This Kingdom was already in the earth in Himself and in the new life He succeeded in creating in those who followed Him. It found itself opposed by physical forces that were injurious to humanity; and these He met fearlessly, sleeping in a storm so violent as to terrify His fisherman companions; and, what is more, He commanded these forces for His Father's purpose in a way that amazed His first followers and is still amazing to us. The reports of His mighty works have to be carefully scrutinized by historical scholars, and no doubt the historicity of some of them is much more fully attested than that of others; but when every allowance is made for the ideas of a prescientific age in which miracles were relatively frequent, and for the possible growth of the marvellous elements in the tradition, enough remains to show that here was a Personality whose power cannot be limited by our usual standards of human ability. Judged by past or present conceptions of what is natural, His works were supernatural; He Himself regarded them as the breaking into the world through Him of the new order that was to be. He discouraged men's craving for the physically miraculous, and thought little of the faith in Him produced by its display; but there can be no question of His extraordinary control of physical forces for the aims of His Kingdom. It was, however, in the moral conflict between the Divine Order and things as they were, that He saw the decisive collision, and faced it with heroic faith in His Father's victory. When the dominant authorities in Church and State were about to crush Him, He looked forward undismayed, and in the glowing pictures of fervent Jewish men of hope He imaged the Divine Rule He proclaimed coming in power.

He was to His followers the Conqueror of sin. He went forth to wage war with evil in the world, because He was conscious that He had first bound the strong man, and could spoil his house. In an autobiographical parable He seems to have told them something of His own battle with temptation and of His victory. They found in

Him One who both shamed and transformed them; they saw Him forgiving and altering sinners; and, above all, His cross, from the earliest days when they began to ask themselves what it meant, had for them redemptive force.

He was to them the Victor of death. However the historian may deal with the details of the narratives of the appearances of the risen Jesus to His disciples, he cannot fail to recognize the conviction of Jesus' followers that their Lord had returned to them and was alive with power. We must remember that it was to faith alone that the risen Jesus showed Himself, and that no one outside the circle of believers (unless we except Saul of Tarsus) saw Him after His death. Historical research, independent of Christian faith, may not be able positively to affirm the correctness of the Easter faith of the disciples, for the data lie, in part at least, outside the range of such research. But the historian must leave the door open for faith; and he may go further and point out that faith's explanation best fits the facts. Present faith finds itself prepared to receive the witness of the men of faith centuries ago.

The attempt to banish Jesus from our world signally failed; He was a more living and potent force in it after, than before, His death.

This singular religious experience, character and victory we ascribe to the Jesus of history through the tradition which preserves for us His religious impression upon His immediate followers. There are some who lay little stress upon the events of the past; like Shelley's Skylark, they are "scorners of the ground." Why, they ask, should we care what took place in Palestine centuries ago? The answer is that it is the roots which go down into historic fact which give the whole tree of Christian faith its stability and vigor. A tree gathers nourishment and grows by its leaves; and Christianity has undoubtedly taken into itself many enriching elements from the life about it in every age; but a tree without roots is neither sturdy nor alive. A Christianity which disregards its origin in the Jesus of genuine memory may label anything "Christian" that it fancies, and end by losing its own identity; and a Christianity which does not constantly keep learning of the Jesus of the New Testament, and renewing its convictions, ideals and purposes from Him, ceases to be vital. We do not think of Christianity as a fixed quantity or an unchanging essence, but as a life; and life is ever growing and changing. But with all its growth and change it keeps true to type, and the type is Jesus Christ. The gospels, which conserve the impress of that Life upon men of faith, are anchors in the actual amid windy storms of speculation. We are not constructing a Christ out of our spiritual experiences, but letting Him who gave life to these early followers, through their memories of Him, recreate us into His and their fellowship with God and man.

Their spiritual experiences are the sensitive plate which caught and kept for all time the image of the historic Jesus; but their experience is a memory, and there must be a further experience in us upon which this memory throws and fixes His image before we know Jesus Christ for ourselves. Unless a man's soul is unimpressionable, he cannot be faced with the Christ of the New Testament without being deeply affected. "We needs must love the highest when we see it," and to millions throughout the earth Jesus is their highest inspiration. For them He ceases to belong to the past and becomes their most significant Contemporary. They do not look back to Him; they look up to Him as their present Comrade and Lord; and in loyalty to Him they find themselves possessed of a new life.

In a previous chapter, we used the phrase "man's response to his highest inspirations" as a description of religious experience; and in responding to the appeal of Jesus, His followers pass into the characteristically Christian experience of the Divine—an experience which involves two main elements: communion through Jesus with God, and communion with Jesus in God.

Communion through Jesus with God. His singular religious experience they find themselves sharing to some degree. They repeat His discoveries in the unseen and corroborate them. God, the God and Father of Jesus Christ, becomes their God and Father, with thom they live in the trust and love and obedience of children. And for them Jesus' consciousness of God becomes *authoritative.* It is not that they consider

Him in possession of secret sources of information inaccessible to them, but that, incomparably more expert, He has penetrated farther and more surely into the unseen, and they trustfully follow Him. He does not lord it over them as servants, but leads them as His friends. "Man," says Keats, in a remark which illustrates Jesus' method with His disciples, "Man should not dispute or assert, but whisper results to his neighbor." He, who of old did not strive nor cry aloud, still so quietly gives those who obey Him His attitude towards God, that they scarcely realize how much they owe Him. Only here and there a discerning follower, like Luther, is aware how all-important is the contribution that comes through a conscious sharing of Christ's revelation, "Whosoever loses Christ, all faiths (of the Pope, the Jews, the Turks, the common rabble) become one faith."

And when once Jesus is authoritative for a man, He is the *supreme* religious authority. A tolerant Roman, like Alexander Severus, set statues of Apollonius, Christ, Abraham, Orpheus, "and others of that sort," in his lararium; and many today are inclined to make a similar religious combination. Where Christ is concerned, there can be for His followers no other "of that sort." We cherish every discovery of the Divine by any saint of any faith which does not conflict with the revelation of Jesus; but to those who have found Him the Way to the Father, His consciousness of God is decisive. In the margin of his copy of Bacon's *Essays,* William Blake wrote opposite some statement of that worldly-wiseman, "This is certain: if what Bacon says is true, what Christ says is false." A loyal Christian must set every opinion he meets as clearly in the light of his Lord's mind, and choose accordingly his course in the seen and in the unseen.

When through Jesus we are in fellowship with His God, Jesus Himself becomes to us *the revelation of God.* The Deity to whom we are led through His faith discloses Himself to us in Jesus' character. What we call Divine, as we worship it in One whom we picture in the heavens or indwelling within us, we discover at our side in Jesus; and if we are impelled to speak of the Deity of the Father, when we characterize our highest inspirations from the unseen, we cannot do

less than speak of the Deity of the Son,
through whom in the seen these same inspirations pass to us. Jesus Himself awakens in
us a religious response. We instinctively
adore Him, devote our all to Him, trust
Him with a confidence as complete as we
repose in God. We are either idolaters, or
Jesus is the unveiling in a human life of the
Most High; He is to us God manifest in the
flesh.

And Jesus is also *the revelation of what
man may become.* None ever had a sublimer
faith in man than He who dared bid His followers be perfect as their Father is perfect.
He did not close His eyes to men's glaring
unlikeness to God; He said to His auditors,
"ye being evil"; He believed in the necessity
of their complete transformation through
repentance. But when He asked them to
follow Him, He set no limits to the distance
they would be able to go. He did not warn
them that they must stop at the foot of Calvary, while He climbed to the top; or that
they could not go with Him in His intimacy
with the Father. Some Christians, out of
reverence for Jesus, think it necessary to
draw a sharp line between Him and our-

selves, and remind us that we cannot over-
pass it; but He drew no such line. He
believed in the divine possibilities of divinely
changed men. As a matter of fact we find
ourselves immeasurably beneath Him, and,
the more we long to be like Him, the greater
the distance between us seems to become.
But He is as confident that He can conform
us to His likeness, as that He Himself is
at one with His Father.

It is worth emphasizing that this Personality in whom we find the revelation of God
and the ideal of manhood is a figure in history. When an apostle was speaking of
"the one Mediator between God and men,"
he laid stress on the fact that He was "Himself *man.*" When a distinction is drawn
between the Christ of experience and the
Christ of history, we must not be confused.
The content of the name "Jesus" was given
once for all in the impression made by the
Man of Nazareth, One made "in all points"
like ourselves. We may understand Him
better than those who knew Him in the flesh;
we may see the bearing of His life on many
situations that were entirely beyond even
His ken; and so we may have "a larger

Christ," exactly as succeeding generations
sometimes form truer estimates of men than
contemporaries; but all that is authentic in
our "larger Christ" was implicit in the Man
of Galilee. That to which we respond as to
God is the historic Jesus mirrored in His
disciples' faith. We agree with the eloquent
words of Tertullian: "We say, and before
all men we say, and torn and bleeding under
your tortures we cry out, 'We worship God
through Christ. Count Christ a man, if you
please; by Him and in Him God would be
known and adored.'" And our assurance
that we can become like Jesus rests on the
fact that this life has been already lived. A
mountain top, however lofty, we can hope to
scale, for it is part of the same earth on
which we stand; but a star, however alluring,
we have no confidence of reaching. Jesus'
worth as an example to us lies in our finding
in Him "ideal manhood closed in real
man."

In fellowship through Jesus with God we
discover that His victory is vicarious; He
conquered for Himself *and for us* the world
and sin and death.

He imparts His faith in the coming of

the Divine Order in the world. His followers share His fearless and masterful attitude towards physical forces; when they appear opposed to God's purpose of love, the Christian is confident that they are not inherently antagonistic to it: "to them that love God all things work together for good." What is called "nature" is not something fixed, but plastic; something which can be conformed to the will of the God and Father of Jesus. A pestilential Panama, for instance, is not natural, but subnatural, and must be brought up to its divine nature, when it will serve the children of God. The Rule of God in nature, like the Kingdom in Jesus' parables, must both be awaited patiently—for it will require advances in men's consciences and knowledge to control physical forces in the interest of love—and striven for believingly. And even when bitter circumstances seem, whether only for the present or permanently, inescapable, when pain and disaster and death must be borne, the Christian accepts them as part of the loving and wise will of God, as his Lord acquiesced in His own suffering: "The cup which the Father hath given Me, shall I not drink it?"

And Jesus confers His confidence in the alterability of the world of human relations. Christians believe in the superiority of moral over material forces, in the wisdom and might of love. A life like Christ's is pronounced in every generation unpractical, until under His inspiration some follower lives it; and slowly, as in His own case, its success is acclaimed. His principles, as applied to an economic institution such as slavery, or to the treatment of the criminal, are counted visionary, until, constrained by His Spirit, men put them into practice, and their results gradually speak for themselves. His followers in every age have seemed fools to many, if not to most, of their judicious contemporaries; but cheered by His confidence, they venture on apparently hopeless undertakings, and find that He has overcome the world.

Jesus' victory over sin works in true disciples a similar conquest. Christians label any unchristlikeness sin, and they vastly darken the world with a new sense of its evil, and are themselves most painfully aware of their own sinfulness. Jesus' conscience has creative power, and reproduces its sensitive-

ness in theirs; they are born into a life of new
sympathies and obligations and penitences.
By His faith, and supremely by His cross,
He communicates to His followers the assurance of God's forgiveness which reëstablishes
their intercourse with Him, and releases His
life in them; and Jesus lays them under a
new and more potent compulsion to live no
longer unto themselves, but unto their
brethren.

Jesus' conquest of death is to His followers the vindication of His faith in God,
and God's attestation of Him; and with such
a God Lord of heaven and earth, death has
neither sting nor victory; it cannot separate
from God's love; and it is itemized among a
Christian's assets. The face of death has
been transfigured. Aristides, explaining the
Christian faith about the year 125 A.D.,
writes, "And if any righteous man among
them passes from the world, they rejoice and
offer thanks to God; and they escort his
body as if he were setting out from one place
to another near." Christians speak of their
dead as "in Christ"—under His all-sufficient
control.

Communion with Jesus in God. When

the Christian through Jesus finds himself in
fellowship with His God and Father, he
does not leave Jesus behind as One whose
work is done. He discovers that he can
maintain this fellowship only as he constantly places himself in such contact with
the historic Figure that God can through
Him renew the experience. It is by going
back to Jesus that we go up to the Father;
or rather, it is through the abiding memory
of Jesus in the world that God reaches down
and lifts us to Himself. And at such times
no Christian thinks of Jesus as a memory,
but as a living Friend. To Him he ad-
dresses himself directly in prayer and praise,
which would be meaningless were there no
present communication between Jesus and
His disciples.

We cannot say that we have an experience
of communion with Jesus which is distin-
guishable from our experience of communion with God; we respond through Jesus to
God. But if our God be the God of Jesus,
we cannot think of Jesus as anywhere in the
universe out of fellowship with Him. His
God would not be Himself, nor would Jesus
be Himself, were the fellowship between

Them interrupted; and we cannot think of ourselves as in touch with the One, without being at the same time in touch with the Other. It is an apparently inevitable inference from our Christian experience, when we attempt to rationalize it, that "our fellowship is with the Father, and with His Son Jesus Christ." In communion with God we are in a society which includes the Father and all His true sons and daughters, the living here and the living yonder, for all live unto Him. They are ours in God; and Jesus supremely, because He is the Mediator of our life with God, is ours in His and our Father.

We have already passed over into the division of our subject which we called *the Christ of reflection.* All experience contains an intellectual element, and we never experience "facts" apart from the ideas in which we represent them to ourselves. But there is a further mental process when we attempt to combine what we think we have experienced in some relationship with all else that we know, and reach a unified view of existence. For example, when Paul took the gospel out of its local setting in Palestine,

and carried it into the Roman world, he had
to interpret the figure of Jesus to set it in
the minds of men who thought in terms very
different from those of the fishermen of
Galilee or the scribes at Jerusalem. Similarly John, who wrote his gospel for Gentile
readers, could not introduce Jesus to them
as the Messiah, and catch their interest; he
took an idea, as common in the thought of
that day as Evolution is in our own—the
Logos or Word, in whom God expresses
Himself and through whom He acts upon
the world—and used that as a point of contact with the minds of his readers. We have
to connect the Christ of our experience with
our thought of God and of the universe.
Three chief questions suggest themselves to
us: How shall we picture Jesus' present life?
How shall we account for His singular personality? How shall we conceive the union
in Him of the Divine and the human, which
we have discovered?

The first of these questions faced the disciples when Jesus was no longer with them
in the flesh. When a cloud received Him
out of their sight, it did not take Him out
of their fancy; finding themselves still in

communion with Him, they had to imagine His present existence with God and with them. They used their current symbol for God—the Most High enthroned above His world—and they pictured Jesus as seated at the right hand of the throne of God. Or they took some vivid metaphor of personal friendship—a figure knocking at the door and entering to eat with them—and found that a fitting interpretation of their experience. These were picturesque ways of saying that Jesus shares God's life and ours. While our current modes of representing the Divine do not localize heaven, the symbolic language of the Bible has so entered into our literature, that in worship and in devout thought we find the New Testament metaphors most satisfactory to express our faith.

The second question was asked even during Jesus' lifetime—"Whence hath this Man these things?" The New Testament writers deal with the question of Jesus' origin in a variety of ways. The earliest of our present gospels opens its narrative with the descent of the Spirit upon Jesus as He answers John's summons to baptism. It seems to

explain His uniqueness by the extraordinary
spiritual endowment bestowed upon Him in
manhood. The first and third gospels contain besides this two other traditions: they
introduce Jesus as the descendant of a line
of devout progenitors, going back in the one
case to David and Abraham, and in the
other still further through Adam to God.
They bring forward His spiritual heredity
as one factor to account for Him. Side by
side with this they place a narrative which
records His birth, not as the Son of Joseph
through whom His ancestry is traced, but
of the Holy Spirit and a virgin-mother.
This gives prominence to the Divine and
human parentage which brought Him into
the world. In Paul and John and the *Epistle to the Hebrews,* there is incarnate in
Jesus a preëxistent heavenly Being—the
Man from heaven, the Word who was from
the beginning with God, the Son through
whom He made the worlds. They present
us with a Divine Being made a man. This
last conception is not combined by any New
Testament writer with a virgin-birth. When
our New Testament books were put together, the Church found all four statements

in its Canon, and combined them (although some of them are not easily combined) in its account of Jesus' origin.

Historical scholars have difficulty in tracing any of these accounts but the first directly to Jesus Himself; but they come from the earliest period of the Church, and they have satisfied many generations of thoughtful Christians as explanations of the uniqueness of the Person of their Lord. Some of them do not seem to be as helpful to modern believers, and are even said to render Him less intelligible. We must beware on the one hand of insisting too strongly that a believer in Jesus Christ shall hold a particular view of His origin; the diversity in the New Testament presentations of Christ would not be there, if all its writers considered all four of these statements necessary in every man's conception of his Lord. And on the other hand, we must point out that it is a tribute to Jesus' greatness that so many circumstances were appealed to to account for Him, and that all of them have spiritual value. All four insist that Jesus' origin is in God, and that in Jesus we find the Divine in the human. All four—a spiritual endow-

ment, a spiritual heredity, a spiritual birth,
the incarnation of God in Man—may well
seem congruous with the Jesus of our experience, even if we are not intellectually satisfied with the particular modes in which these
affirmations have been made in the past. The
question of Jesus' origin is not of primary
importance; He Himself judged nothing by
its antecedents, but by its results—"By their
fruits ye shall know them." No man, today,
should be hindered from believing in Christ,
because he does not find a particular statement in connection with His origin credible.
Christ is here in our world, however He
entered it, and can be tested for what He *is*.
To know Him is not to know how He came
to be, but what He can do for us. "To know
Christ," Melancthon well said, "is to know
His benefits."

The third question, How are we to conceive of the union of Deity and humanity in
Him? is a problem which exercised the
Fourth, Fifth and Sixth Centuries of the
Christian Church to the exclusion of almost
all others. The theologians of those times
worked out (and fought out) the theory of
the union of two "natures" in one "Person,"

which remains the official statement of the Church's interpretation of Christ in Greek, Roman and Protestant creeds. But the philosophy which dealt in "natures" and "persons" is no longer the mode of thought of educated people; and while we may admire the mental skill of these earlier theologians, and may recognize that an Athanasius and his orthodox allies were contending for a vital element in Christian experience, their formulations do not satisfy our minds.

In the last century some divines advanced a modification of this ancient theory, naming it the Kenotic or Self-emptying Theory, from the Greek word used by St. Paul in the phrase, "He *emptied* Himself." The eternal Son of God is represented as laying aside whatever attributes of Deity—omnipresence, omniscience, omnipotence, etc.— could not be manifested in an entirely human life. The Jesus of history *reveals* so much of God as man can contain, but *is* Himself more. But we know of no personality which can lay aside memory, knowledge, etc. The theory begins with a conception of Deity apart from Jesus, and then proceeds to treat Him as partially disclosing this Deity in His

human life; but the Christian has his experience of the Divine through Jesus, and his
reflection must start with Deity as revealed
in Him.

Still later in the century, Albrecht Ritschl
gave another interpretation of Christ's
Person. He began with the completely human Figure of history, and pointed out that
it is through Him we experience communion
with God, so that to His followers Jesus
is divine; His humanity is the medium
through which God reveals Himself to us.
This affirmation of His Deity is an estimate,
made by believers, of Jesus' worth to them;
they cannot prove it to any who are without
a sense of Christ's value as their Saviour.
Any further explanation of how the human
and the Divine are joined in Jesus, he
deemed beyond the sphere of religious
knowledge.

Our modern thought of God as immanent
in His world and in men enables us, perhaps
more easily than some of our predecessors,
to fit the figure of Christ into our minds.
The discovery of the Divine in the human
does not surprise us. We think of God as
everywhere manifesting Himself, but His

presence is limited by the medium in which
it is recognized. He reveals as much of
Himself through nature as nature can disclose; as much through any man as he can
contain; as much through the complete Man
as He is capable of manifesting. Nor does
this Self-revelation of God in Jesus do away
for us with Jesus' own attainment of His
character. Immanent Deity does not sub-
merge the human personality. Jesus was no
merely passive medium through which God
worked, but an active Will who by constant
coöperation with the Father "was perfected." If there was an "emptying," there
was also a "filling," so that we see in Him
the fulness of God. How He alone of all
mankind came so to receive the Self-giving
Father remains for us, as for our predecessors, the ultimate riddle, a riddle akin to that
which makes each of us "indescribably himself." And as for the origin of His unique
Person, we have no better explanations to
substitute for those of the First Century;
the mystery of our Lord's singular personality remains unsolved.

While our reflections almost necessarily
end in guesses, or in impenetrable obscuri-

ties, our experience of Christ's worth can advance to ever greater certainty. We follow Him, and find Him the Way, the Truth and the Life. We trust Him and prove His power to save unto the uttermost. We come to feel that no phrase applied to Him in the New Testament is an exaggeration; our own language, like St. Paul's, admits its inadequacy by calling Him God's *"unspeakable gift."* We see the light of the knowledge of the glory of God in His face; He is to us the Light of life; and we live and strive to make Him the Light of the world. Though we may never be able to reason out to our satisfaction how God and man unite in Him, we discover in Him the God who redeems us and the Man we aspire to be. Jesus is to us (to borrow a saying of Lancelot Andrewes') "God's as much as He can send; ours as much as we can desire."

CHAPTER IV

GOD

The word "God" is often employed as
though it had a fixed meaning. His part in
an event or His relation to a movement is
discussed with the assumption that all who
speak have in mind the same Being. "God"
is the name a man gives to his highest inspiration, and men vary greatly in that which
inspires them. One man's god is his belly,
another's his reputation, a third's clever-
ness. Napoleon reintroduced the cult of
the God of authority, by establishing the
Concordat with Rome, because as he bluntly
put it, "men require to be kept in order."
A number of socially minded thinkers, of
whom the best known is George Eliot, deified humanity and gave themselves to worship and serve it. "Whatever thy heart
clings to and relies on," wrote Luther, "that
is properly thy God." A Christian is one
who clings to Him in whom Jesus trusted,
one who responds to the highest inspirations

of Jesus of Nazareth. And a glance over
Church history leaves one feeling that few
Christians, even among careful thinkers,
have had thoroughly Christian ideas of God.

A principal fault has been the method
used in arriving at the thought of God. Men
began with what was termed "Natural Religion." They studied the universe and in-
ferred the sort of Deity who made and ruled
it. It was intricately and wisely designed;
its God must be omniscient. It was vast;
He must be omnipotent. It displayed the
same orderliness everywhere; He must be
omnipresent. In epochs when men emphasized the beneficence of nature—its beauty,
its usefulness, its wisdom—they concluded
that its Creator was good. In an epoch,
like the latter part of the Nineteenth Century, they drew a very different conclusion.
Charles Darwin wrote, "What a book a
Devil's chaplain might write on the clumsy,
wasteful, blundering, low and horribly cruel
works of nature."

Christians never stopped with the view of
God drawn from "Natural Religion." They
made this their basis, and then added to it
the God of "Revealed Religion," contained

in the Bible. They selected all the texts that
spoke of God, drawing them from *Leviticus*
and *Ecclesiastes* as confidently as from the
gospels and St. Paul, and constructed a
Biblical doctrine of God, which they added
to the omnipotent, omniscient, omnipresent
Being of their inferences from Nature. The
God and Father of Jesus was thus combined
with various, often much lower thoughts of
Deity in the Bible, and then further ob-
scured by the Deity of the current views of
physical and human nature. It is not surprising that few Christians possessed a truly
Christian view of God.

Loyalty to Jesus compels us to begin with
Him. If He is the Way, we are not justi-
fied in taking half a dozen other roads, and
using Him as one path among many. We
ask ourselves what was the highest inspiration of Jesus, what was the Being to whom
He responded with His obedient trust and
with whom He communed. We are eager
not to fashion an image of Divinity for ourselves, which is idolatry as truly when our
minds grave it in thought as when our hands
shape it in stone; but to receive God's disclosure of Himself with a whole-hearted re-

sponse, and interpret, as faithfully as we can, the impression He makes upon us. "God," writes Tyndal, the martyr translator of our English New Testament, "is not man's imagination, but that only which He saith of Himself." Our highest inspirations come to us from Jesus, and He is, therefore, God's Self-unveiling to us, God's "Frankness," His Word made flesh.

Responding to God through Jesus, Christians discover:

First, that God is their Christlike Father, and that He is love as Jesus experienced His love and Himself was love.

Second, that God is the Lord of heaven and earth. We do not know whether He is omniscient, omnipotent, omnipresent; there is much that leads us to think that He is limited. He can do no more than Love can do with His children, and Love has its defeats, and crosses, and tragedies. But trusting the Christlike Father we more and more discover that He is sufficiently in control over all things to accomplish through them His will. He needs us to help Him master nature, and transform it into the servant of man,—to control disease, to harness electricity, to understand earthquakes; and He needs us to help Him conquer human nature and conform it to the likeness of His Son. God's complete lordship waits until His will is done in earth as it is in heaven; but for the present we believe that He is wise and strong enough not to let nature or men defeat His purpose; that He is controlling all things so that they work together for good unto them that love Him.

And third, that God is the indwelling Spirit. The Christlike Father Lord, whom we find outside ourselves through the faith and character of Jesus, becomes as we enter into fellowship with Him, a Force within us. He is the Conscience of our consciences, the Wellspring of motives and impulses and sympathies. We repeat, today, in some degree, the experience of the first disciples at Pentecost; we recognize within ourselves the inspiring, guiding and energizing Spirit of love.

While we find God primarily through Jesus, He reveals Himself to us in many other ways: in the Scriptures, where the generations before us have garnered their experiences of Him; in living epistles in Chris-

tian men and women, and in some who do
not call themselves by the Christian name,
but whose lives disclose the Spirit of God
who was in Jesus; in non-Christian faiths,
where God has always given some glimpse
of Himself in answer to men's search. Christ
is not for us confining but defining; He gives
us in Himself the test to assay the Divine.

Nor do experiences which we label religious exhaust the list of our contacts with
God. Our sense of duty, whether we connect it with God or not, brings us in touch
with Him. Many persons are unconsciously
serving God through their obedience to conscience. It was said of the French *savant,*
Littré, that he was a saint who did not believe in God. He made the motto of his
life, "To love, to know, to serve"; and no
intelligent follower of Him who said, "Inas-
much as ye did it unto one of My brethren,
even these least, ye did it unto Me," will fail
to admit that in such a life there is a genuine,
though unrecognized communion with God.
In our own day when conscience is erecting
new standards of responsibility, rendering
intolerable many things good people have
put up with, demonstrating the horror and

hatefulness of war and forcing us to probe its causes and motives, discontenting us with our industrial arrangements, our business practices, our social order, God is giving us a larger and better Ideal, a fuller vision of Himself. We know what our Christlike Father is in Jesus; but we shall appreciate and understand Him infinitely better as He becomes embodied in the principles and ideals that dominate every home, and trade, and nation.

Again, our perception of beauty affords us a glimpse of God. The Greeks embodied loveliness in their statues of the Divine, because through the satisfaction which came to them from such exquisite figures their souls were soothed and uplifted. They have left on record how the calm and majestic expression of a face carved by a Phidias quieted, charmed, strengthened them. Dion Chrysostom says of the figure of the Olympian Zeus, "Whosoever among mortal men is most utterly toil-worn in spirit, having drunk the cup of many sorrows and calamities, when he stands before this image, methinks, must utterly forget all the terrors and woes of this mortal life." The Greek

Christian fathers often tell us that the same
sense of the infinitely Fair, which was roused
in them by such sights, recurred in a higher
degree when their thoughts dwelt upon the
life and character of Jesus.   Clement of
Alexandria says, "He is so lovely as to be
alone loved by us, whose hearts are set on the
true beauty."   Our æsthetic and our religious experiences often merge; our response
to beauty, whether in nature, or music, or
a painting, becomes a response to God.
Wordsworth says of a lovely landscape that
had stamped its views upon his memory:

> Oft in lonely rooms, and mid the din
> Of towns and cities, I have owed to them,
> In hours of weariness, sensations sweet,
> Felt in the blood, and felt along the heart;
> And passing even into my purer mind
> With tranquil restoration:—feelings too
> Of unremembered pleasure; such, perhaps,
> As have no slight or trivial influence
> On that best portion of a good man's life,
> His little, nameless, unremembered acts
> Of kindness and of love.

Shelley, while insistently denying or defy-
ing all the gods of accepted religion, finds
himself adoring

> that Beauty
> Which penetrates and clasps and fills the world,
> Scarce visible for extreme loveliness.

Surely the God Christians adore is in these experiences, though men know it not. St. Augustine believed that "all that is beautiful comes from the highest Beauty, which is God." They who begin with the cult of Beauty may have a conception of the Divine that has nothing to do with, or is even opposed to, the God and Father of Jesus; but when His God is supreme, inspirations from all things lovely may vastly supplement our thought of Him. "Music on earth much light upon heaven has thrown."

Science, too, has its contribution to offer to our thought of Him who is over all and through all and in all. Truth is one, and scientific investigation and religious experience are two avenues that lead to the one Reality faith names God. Science of itself can never lead us beyond visible and tangible facts; but its array of facts may suggest to faith many things about the invisible Father, the Lord of all. Present-day science with its emphasis upon continuity makes us think of a God who is no occasional visitor, but everywhere and always active; its conception of evolution brings home to us the patient and longsuffering labor of a Father who worketh even until now; its stress upon law reminds us that He is never capricious but reliable; its practical mastery of forces, like those which enable men to use the air or to navigate under the water, recalls to us the old command to subdue the earth as sons of God, and adds the new responsibility to use our control, as the Son of God always did, in love's cause.

Philosophy, too, which Professor James has described as "our more or less dumb sense of what life honestly and deeply means," helps us to make clear our idea of God. A philosopher is just a thoughtful person who takes the discoveries that his religious, moral, æsthetic, scientific experiences have brought home, and tries to set in order all he knows of truth, beauty, right, God.

In attempting to philosophize upon their discoveries of God, Christian thinkers have arrived at the doctrine of the Trinity in Unity. It was, first, an attempt to hold fast to the great foundation truth of the Old

Testament that God is One. The world in which Christianity found itself had a host of deities—a god for the sea and another for the wind, a god of the hearth and a god of the empire, and so on. Today it is only too easy to obey one motive in the home and another in one's business, to follow one principle in private life and another in national life, and to be polytheists again. Christian faith insists that "there is one God, the Father, of whom are all things and we unto Him." We adore One who is Christlike love, and we will serve no other. We trust Christlike love as the divine basis for a happy family life, and also for successful commerce, for statesmanlike international dealings, for the effective treatment of every political and social question. The inspirations that come to us from a glorious piece of music or from an heroic act of self-sacrifice, from some new discovery or from a novel sensitiveness of conscience, are all inspirations from the one God. At every moment and in every situation we must keep the same fundamental attitude towards life —trustful, hopeful, serving—because in every experience, bitter or sweet, we are always in touch with the one Lord of all, our Christlike Father.

In this Unity Christians have spoken of a Trinity. Paul summing up the blessing of God, speaks of "the grace of our Lord Jesus Christ, and the love of God, and the communion of the Holy Spirit." He says, "through Jesus we have our access in one Spirit unto the Father." He and his fellow believers had been redeemed from selfishness to love, from slavery to freedom; and they accounted for their new life by saying that, through the grace of Jesus, they had come to experience the fatherly love of God, and to find His Spirit binding them in a brotherhood of service for one another and the world. The New Testament goes no further: it states these experiences of Jesus, of God, of the Spirit; but it does not tell us the exact relations of the Three—how God is related to the Spirit, or Jesus distinct and at the same time one with the Father. So acute a thinker as Paul never seems to have worked this out. At one time he compares God's relation to His Spirit to man's relation to his spirit ("Who among men knoweth the things of a man, save the spirit of the man which is in him? even so the things of God none knoweth, save the Spirit of God") ; and once he identifies the Spirit with the glorified Christ ("The Lord is the Spirit").

But while Paul and other New Testament writers did not feel the need of thinking out what their threefold experience of God implied as to His Being, later Christians did; and using the terms of the current Greek philosophy, they elaborated the conception of three "Persons" in one Godhead. We have no exact equivalent in English for the Greek word which is translated "person" in this definition. It is not the same as "a person" for that would give us three gods; nor is it something impersonal, a mode or aspect of God. It is something in between a personality and a personification.

Let us remember that this doctrine is not in the New Testament, but is an attempt to explain certain experiences that are ascribed in the New Testament to Jesus, the Father, the Holy Spirit. Even the hardiest thinkers caution us that our knowledge of God is limited to a knowledge of His relations to us: Augustine says, "the workings of the

Trinity are inseparable," and Calvin, com-
menting on a passage whose "aim is shortly
to sum up all that is lawful for men to know
of God," notes that it is "a description, not
of what He is in Himself, but of what He
is to us, that our knowledge of Him may
stand rather in a lively perception, than in
a vain and airy speculation." But let us
also recall that in this doctrine generations
of Christians have conserved indispensable
elements in their thought of God:—His
fatherhood, His Self-disclosure in Christ,
His spiritual indwelling in the Christian
community. Wherever it has been cast
aside, something vitalizing to Christian life
has gone with it. But at present it is not
a doctrine of much practical help to many
religious people; and it often constitutes a
hindrance to Jews and Mohammedans, and
to some born within the Church in their
endeavor to understand and have fellowship with the Christian God.

We may adopt one of two attitudes
towards it: we may accept it blindly as "a
mystery" on the authority of the long centuries of Christian thought, which have used
it to express their faith in God—hardly a

Protestant or truly Christian position which bids us "Prove all things; hold fast that which is good"; or we may consider it reverently as the attempt of the Christian Church of the past to interpret its discovery of God as the Father Lord, revealed in Christ, and active within us as the Spirit of love; and use it in so far as it makes our experience richer and clearer, remembering that it is only a man-made attempt to interpret Him who passeth understanding. The important matter is not the orthodoxy of our doctrine, but the richness of our personal experience of God. Dr. Samuel Johnson said: "We all *know* what light is; but it is not so easy to *tell* what it is." Christians know, at least in part, what God is; but it is far from easy to state what He is; and each age must revise and say in its own words what God means to it. Here is a statement in which generations of believers have summed up their intercourse with the Divine. Have we entered into the fulness of their fellowship with God?

Do we know Him as our Father? This does not mean merely that we accept the idea of His kinship with our spirits and trust His

kindly disposition towards us; but that we
let Him establish a direct line of paternity
with us and father our impulses, our
thoughts, our ideals, our resolves. Jesus'
sonship was not a relation due to a past
contact, but to a present connection. He
kept taking His Being, so to speak, again
and again from God, saying, "Not as I will,
but as Thou wilt." His every wish and
motive had its heredity in the Father whom
He trusted with childlike confidence, and
served with a grown son's intelligent and
willing comradeship. Fatherhood meant to
Jesus authority and affection; obedience and
devotion on His part maintained and perfected His sonship.

Further, we cannot, according to Jesus, be
in sonship with this Father save as we are in
true brotherhood with all His children. God
is (to employ a colloquial phrase) "wrapped
up" in His sons and daughters, and only as
we love and serve them, are we loving and
serving Him. In Jesus' summary of the
Law He combined two apparently conflict-
ing obligations, when He said, "Thou shalt
love the Lord thy God with *all* thy heart,
and thou shalt love thy neighbor." If a man

loves God with his all, how can there be any
remainder of love to devote to someone else?
What we do for any man—the least, the last,
the lost,—we do for God. We do not know
Him as Father, until we possess the obligat-
ing sense of our kinship with all mankind,
and say, *"Our* Father."

Do we know God in the Son? There is a
sense in which Jesus is the "First Person"
in the Christian Trinity. Our approach to
God begins with Him. In St. Paul's familiar benediction, the grace of our Lord Jesus
Christ precedes the love of God. We know
God's love only as we experience the grace
of Jesus. We cannot experience that grace
except as we let Jesus be Lord. Absolute
and entire self-commitment to Him allows
Him to renew us after His own likeness and
equip us for service in His cause. He cannot
transform a partially devoted life, nor use a
half-dedicated man. Those who yield Him
lordship, treating Him as God by giving
Him their adoring trust and complete obedience, discover His Godhood. To them He
proves Himself, by all that He accomplishes
in and through them, worthy of their fullest

devotion and reverence. He becomes to
them God manifest in a human life.

While in the order of our experience Jesus
comes first, as we follow Him, He makes
Himself always second. He points us from
Himself to the Father, like Himself and
greater; "My Father is greater than I."
There is a remoteness, as well as a nearness,
in God; it is His "greaterness" which gives
worth to His likeness. To use a philosophical phrase, only the transcendent God can
be truly immanent. We prize Immanuel—
God *with* us, because through Him we climb
to God *above* us. Jesus is the Way; but no
one wishes to remain forever en route; he
arrives; and home is the Father. Jesus is
the image of the invisible God; but the
image on the retina of our eye is not something on which we dwell; we see through it
the person with whom we are face to face.
We know God our Father in His Son.
Every aspect of Jesus' character unveils for
us an aspect of the character of the Lord
of heaven and earth. Every experience
through which Jesus passed in His life with
men suggests to us an experience through
which our Father is passing with us His

children. The cross on Calvary is a picture of the age-long and present sacrifice of our God as He suffers with and for us. The open grave is for us the symbol of His unconquerable love, stronger than the world and sin and death. God's embodiment of Himself in this Son, made in all points like ourselves, attests the essential kinship between Him and us—God's humanity and our potential divinity.

Do we know God in the Spirit? His incarnation in Jesus evidences His "incarnability," and His eagerness to have His fulness dwell in every son who will receive Him. To know God in the Spirit is so to follow Jesus that we share His sonship with the Father and have Him abiding in us, working through us His works, manifesting Himself in our mortal lives.

Our Father is the great public Spirit of the universe, the most responsible and responsive Being in existence. The needs of all are claims on His service, their sins are burdens of guilt on His conscience, their joys and woes enlist His sympathy. He has His life in the lives of His children. The Spirit is God's Life in men, God living in them. To possess His will to serve, His sense of obligation, His interest and compassion, is to have the Holy Spirit dwelling and regnant in us. It was so that the Father's Spirit possessed Jesus and made His abode in Him; and the Holy Spirit is the Spirit of the Father and of the Son in the Christian community.

And what a difference it makes whether we feel that the responsibilities our consciences force us to assume, the sympathies in which our hearts go out, the interests we are impelled to take, the resolves and longings and purposes within us, are just our own, or are God's inspirations! If they are simply ours, who knows what will come of them? If they are His, we can yield to them assured that it is God who worketh in us to will and to do of His good pleasure.

Our faith in God as Self-imparting by His Spirit makes possible our confident expectation that He can and will incarnate Himself socially in the whole family of His children, as once He was incarnate in Jesus. Christians who devote themselves to fashioning social relations after the mind of Christ, and inspiring their brethren with His faith and purpose, are conscious that through them the Spirit of God is entering more and more into His world, revealing the Father in the new community of love, which is being born. Sir Edward Burne-Jones once wrote: "That was an awful word of Ruskin's, that artists paint God for the world. There's a lump of greasy pigment at the end of Michael Angelo's hog-bristle brush, and by the time it has been laid on the stucco, there is something there, that all men with eyes recognize as Divine. Think what it means: it is the power of bringing God into the world—making God manifest!" Men and women who are molding homes and industries, towns and nations, so that they embody love, and influencing for righteousness the least and lowest of the children of men, are putting before a whole world's eyes the Divine, are helping build the habitation of God in the Spirit. Through them God imparts Himself to mankind.

God over all—the Father to whom we look up with utter trust, and from whom moment by moment we take our lives in obedient devotion; God through all— through Jesus supremely, and through every

child who opens his life to Him with the
willingness of Jesus; God in all—the direct-
ing, empowering, sanctifying Spirit, producing in us characters like Christ's, employ-
ing and equipping us for the work of His
Kingdom, and revealing Himself in a community more and more controlled by love:
this is our Christian thought of the Divine—
"one God and Father of all, who is over all
and through all and in all."

CHAPTER V

THE CROSS

The human life in which succeeding generations have found their picture of God ended in a bloody tragedy. It was a catastrophe which all but wrecked the loyalty of Jesus' little group of followers; it was an event which proved a stumbling block in their endeavor to win their countrymen to their Lord, and which seemed folly to the great mass of outsiders in the Roman world. It was a most baffling circumstance for them to explain either to themselves or to others; but, as they lived on under the control of their Lord's Spirit, this tragedy came gradually to be for them the most richly significant occurrence in His entire history; and ever since the cross has been the distinctive symbol of the Christian faith. It had a variety of meanings for the men of the New Testament; and it has had many more for their followers in subsequent centuries. We are not limited to viewing it through the eyes of others, nor to interpreting it with their thoughts. We are enriched as we try to share their experiences of its power and light; but we must go to Calvary for ourselves, and look at the Crucified with the eyes of our own hearts, and ask ourselves of what that cross convinces us.

Its first and most obvious disclosure is the unchristlikeness, and that means for us the ungodlikeness, of our world. We study the chief actors in this event, and conclude that had we known personally Caiaphas, Annas and Pilate, and even Herod and Judas Iscariot, we should have found them very like men we meet every day, very like ourselves, with a great deal in them to interest, admire and attract. And behind them we scan a crowd of inconspicuous and unnamed persons whose collective feelings and opinions and consciences were quite as responsible for this occurrence, as were the men whose names are linked with it; and they impress us as surprisingly like the public of our own day. It was by no means the lowest elements in the society of that age who took Jesus to the cross; they were among the most devout and conscientious and thoughtful people of their time. Nor was it the worst elements in them which impelled them to class Him as an undesirable, of whom their world ought to be rid; their loyalties and convictions were involved in that judgment. They acted in accord with what was considered the most enlightened and earnest public opinion. We can think of no more high-minded person in Jerusalem than young Saul of Tarsus, the student of Gamaliel; and we know how cordially he approved the course the leaders of Israel had taken in putting Jesus out of the way.

The cross is the point where God and His children, even the best of them, clash. At Calvary we see the rocky coast-line of men's thoughts and feelings against which the incoming tide of God's mind and heart broke; and we hear the moaning of the resisted waves. The crucifixion is the exposure of the motives and impulses, the aspirations and traditions, of human society. Its ungodlikeness is made plain. We get our definition of sin from Calvary; sin is any unlikeness to the Spirit of Christ, revealed supremely in that act of self-sacrifice. The lifeless form of the Son of God on the tree is the striking evidence of the antagonism between the children of men and their Father. Jesus completely represented Him, and this broken body on the gibbet was the inevitable result. Golgotha convinces us of the ruinous forces that live in and dominate our world; it faces us with the suicidal elements in men's spirits that drive them to murder the Christlike in themselves; it tears the veil from each hostile thought and feeling that enacts this tragedy and exposes the God-murdering character of our sin. Sin is deicidal. When that Life of light is extinguished, we find a world about us and within us so dark that its darkness can be felt. The fateful reality of the battle between love and selfishness, knowledge and ignorance, between God and whatever thwarts His purpose, is made plain to us in that pierced and blood-stained Figure on the cross. In the sense of being the victim of the ungodlike forces in human life, Jesus bore sin in His own body on the tree.

A second and equally clear disclosure is that of a marvellous conscience. What takes Jesus Christ to that tragic death? It is perfectly evident that He need not have come

up to Jerusalem and hazarded this issue; He
came of His own accord; and we can think
of dozens of reasons that might have induced
Him to remain in Galilee, going about
quietly and accomplishing all manner of
good. Why did He give up the opportunities of a life that was so incalculably service-
able, and apparently court death? Jesus
was always conscientious in what He did;
He felt Himself bound to the lives about
Him by the firmest cords of obligation, and
whatever He attempted He deemed He
owed men. If there was a Zacchæus
whose honesty and generosity had given way
under the faulty system of revenue-collect-
ing then in vogue, Jesus considered Himself
involved in his moral ruin and obliged to do
what He could to restore him: "I *must* abide
at thy house." If there were sick folk,
their diseases were to Him, in part at least,
morally wrong, devil-caused (to use His
First Century way of explaining what we
ascribe to inherited weakness or to blame-
worthy conditions) ; and demoniacal control
over lives in God's world was something for
which He felt Himself socially accountable:
"*Ought* not this woman, whom Satan hath

bound, to have been loosed?" If the Church
of His day was unable to reach large sections
of the population with its appeal, if it succeeded very imperfectly in making children
of the Most High out of those whom it did
reach, if with its narrowness and bigotry it
made of its converts "children of hell," as
Jesus Himself put it, if it exaggerated trifles
and laid too little stress on justice, mercy
and fidelity, He, as a member of that
Church, was chargeable with its failures, and
must strive to put a new conscience into
God's people: "I *must* preach the good tid-
ings of the Kingdom of God." Ibsen, the
dramatist, wrote to his German translator,
Ludwig Passarge, "In every new poem or
play I have aimed at my own spiritual eman-
cipation and purification—for a man shares
the responsibility and the guilt of the society
to which he belongs." Jesus felt implicated
in all that was not as it should be among the
children of men, and cleared Himself from
complicity with it by setting Himself reso-
lutely to change it. He considered that the
human brotherhood in its sinfulness exacted
nothing less of Him.

It is commonly taught that the Lord's

Prayer is a form that was suggested by
Jesus to His disciples, but that it could not
have been a prayer which He Himself used
with them, because of its plea for forgiveness.
It is true that it is introduced in our Gospels
as provided by the Master for His followers,
"When *ye* pray, say." But millions of
Christians instinctively associate it with
Jesus' own utterances to the Father. And
may they not be correct? "Forgive us *our*
debts," is a social confession of sin, in which
our Lord may well have joined, just as He
underwent John's baptism of repentance,
though Himself sinless, in order to fulfil all
righteousness. He regarded Himself as
indebted; His work, His teaching, His suffering, His death, were not to Him a gift
which He was at liberty to make or to with-
hold. In the "must" so often on His lips we
cannot miss the sense of social obligation.
He was (to borrow suggestive lines of
Shelley's)

> a nerve o'er which do creep
> The else unfelt oppressions of the earth.

They came home to His conscience, and He
could not shake them off. They were so

many claims on Him; He felt He owed the
world a life, and He was ready to pay the
debt to the last drop of His blood. "The
Son of man *must* suffer and be killed." To
the end He cast about for some less awful
way of meeting His obligations. "My
Father, if it be possible, let this cup pass
away from Me." But when no other alternative seemed conscientiously possible to
Him, He went to Golgotha with a sense of
moral satisfaction. *"Ought* not the Christ
to have suffered these things?" Without any
disturbing consciousness of having personally added to the world's evil, with no plea
for pardon for His own sins on His lips but
only for those of others, His conscience was
burdened with the injustice and disloyalties,
the brutalities and failures, of the family of
God, in which He was a Son, and He bore
His brothers' sins on His spirit, and gave
Himself to the utmost to end them.

A third disclosure of the cross is the in-
comparable sympathy of the Victim. How
shall we account for His recoil from the
thought of dying, for His shrinking from
this death as from something which sickened
Him, for the darkness and anguish of His

soul in Gethsemane at the prospect, and for the abysmal sense of forsakenness on the cross? His sensitiveness of heart made Him feel the pain and shame of other men, a pain and shame they were frequently too stolid and obtuse to feel. He could not see able-bodied and willing workmen standing idle in the marketplace because no man had hired them, without sharing their discouragement and bitterness, nor prodigals making fools of themselves without feeling the disgrace of their unfilial folly. His parables are so vivid because He has Himself lived in the experiences of others. *"Cor cordium"* is the inscription placed upon Shelley's grave; and it is infinitely more appropriate for the Man of Nazareth. In His sensitive sympathy we are aware of

> Desperate tides of the whole great world's anguish
> Forc'd through the channels of a single heart.

We cannot account for His recoil from the cross, save as we remember His sense of kinship with those who were reddening their hands with the blood of the Representative of their God. If we have ever stood beside a devoted wife in the hour when her husband

is disgraced, or been in a home where sons
and daughters are overwhelmed with a
mother's shame, we have some faint idea of
how Jesus felt the guilt of His relatives
when they slew Him. He was the conscience
of His less conscientious brethren: "the re-
proaches of them that reproached Thee, fell
on Me." He realized, as they did not, the
enormity of what they were doing. The
utter and hideous ungodlikeness of the world
was expressed for Him in those who would
have none of Him, and cried: "Away with
Him! Crucify, crucify Him." His keen-
ness of conscience and His acute sympathy
brought to His lips the final cry, "My God,
My God, why hast Thou forsaken Me?"
The sinless Sufferer on the cross, in His oneness with His brethren, felt their wrong-
doing His own; acknowledged in His forsakenness that God could have nothing to
do with it, for it was anti-God; confessed
that it inevitably separated from Him and
He felt Himself in such kinship and sympathy with sinning men that He was actually
away from God. "That was hell," said
old Rabbi Duncan, "and He tasted it."

But our minds revolt. We do not believe

that God deserted His Son; on the contrary we are certain that He was never closer to Him. Shall we question the correctness of Jesus' personal experience, and call Him mistaken? We seem compelled either to do violence to His authority in the life of the spirit with God, or to our conviction of God's character. Perhaps there is another alternative. A century ago the physicist, Thomas Young, discovered the principle of the interference of light. Under certain conditions light added to light produces darkness; the light waves interfere with and neutralize each other. Is there not something analogous to this in the sphere of the spirit? Is not every new unveiling of God accompanied by unsettlements and seeming darkenings of the soul, temporary obscurations of the Divine Face? In all our advances in religious knowledge are we not liable to undergo

> Fallings from us, vanishings,
> Blank misgivings of the creature?

And may it not have been God's coming closer than ever to the Son of His love, or rather the Son's coming closer to the Father,

as He entirely shared and expressed God's
own sympathy and conscience, and was made
perfect by the things which He suffered,
that wrought in His sinless soul the awful
blackness of the feeling of abandonment?

In the sense of suffering sin's force, of
conscientiously accepting its burden, of sen-
sitively sympathizing with the guilty, Jesus
bore sin in His own body on the tree.

And, as we stand facing the Crucified, we
cannot escape a sense of personal connection
with that tragedy. The solidarity of the
human family in all its generations has been
brought home to us in countless ways by
modern teachers; we are members one of
another, and as we scan the cross this is a
family catastrophe in which the actors are
our kinsmen, and the blood of the Victim
stains us as sharers of our brothers' crime.
And, further, as we look into the motives of
Christ's murderers—devout Pharisee and
conservative Sadducee, Roman politician
and false friend, bawling rabble and undis-
criminating soldiery, the host of indifferent
or approving faces of the public behind them
—they seem strangely familiar to us. They
have been, they are still, alive by turns in us.

The harmless spark of electricity that greets the touch of one's hand on a metal knob on a winter's day is one with the bolt of lightning that wrecks a giant oak. The selfish impulse, the narrow prejudice, the ignorant suspicion, the callous indifference, the self-satisfied respectability, which frequently dominate us and determine our decisions, are one with that cruel combination of motives which drove the nails in the hands and feet of the Son of God. Still further, the suffering of Jesus never seems to an acute conscience something that happened once, but is over now. The Figure that hung and bled on the tree centuries ago becomes indissolubly joined in our thought with every life today that is the victim of similar misunderstanding and neglect, injustice and brutality; and, while our sense of social responsibility charges us with complicity in all the wrong and woe of our brethren, that haunting Form on Calvary hangs before our eyes, and

> Makes me feel it was my sin,
> As though no other sin there were,
> That was to Him who bears the world
> A load that He could scarcely bear.

We may say to ourselves that this is fanciful, that we were not the Sanhedrin who condemned Jesus, nor the Roman procurator who ordered His execution, nor the scoffing soldiers who carried out his command; but the conscience which the cross itself creates charges us with participation in the murder of the Son of God. That cross becomes an inescapable fact in our moral world, an element in our outlook upon duty, a factor tingeing life with tragic somberness. It forces upon us the conviction that it is all too possible for us to reënact Golgotha, and by doing or failing to do, directly or indirectly, for one of the least of Christ's brethren to crucify Him afresh, and put Him to an open shame.

But if the cross seems to color life somberly, it also gilds it with glory. As we follow Christ, we discover more and more clearly that all which we possess of greatest worth has come to us, and keeps coming to us, through Him. What he endured centuries ago on that hill without the city wall is a wellspring of inspiration flowing up in the purest and finest motives in the life of today. There is a direct line of ancestry from the best principles in the lives of nations, and of men and women about us, running back to Calvary. Day after day we find ourselves and the whole world made different because of that tragic occurrence of the past, shamed out of the motives that caused it, and lifted into the life of the Crucified. A recent dramatist makes the centurion, in the darkness at the foot of the cross, say to Mary: "I tell you, woman, this dead Son of yours, disfigured, shamed, spat upon, has built a Kingdom this day that can never die. The living glory of Him rules it. The earth is *His* and He made it. He and His brothers have been molding and making it through the long ages; they are the only ones who ever really did possess it: not the proud; not the idle; not the vaunting empires of the world. Something has happened up here on this hill today to shake all our kingdoms of blood and fear to the dust. The earth is His, the earth is theirs, and they made it. The meek, the terrible meek, the fierce agonizing meek, are about to enter into their inheritance."

Nor is this all of which that cross convinces us. We find ourselves giving that crucified Man our supreme adoration; He is

for us that which we cannot but worship.
Instinctively and irresistibly we yield Him
our highest reverence, trust and devotion.
As we think out what is involved in the impression He makes upon us, we come to our
conception of His deity; and through Him
we discover ourselves in touch with the Highest there is in the universe, with the Most
High. Calvary becomes, for those who look
trustingly at the Crucified, a window
through which we see into the life of the
Lord of heaven and earth. Jesus' sin-bear-
ing is for us a revelation of the eternal sin-
bearing of the God and Father of us all.
Behind the cross of wood outside the gate of
Jerusalem we catch sight of a vast, age-
enduring cross in the heart of the Eternal,
forced on Him generation after generation
by His children's unlikeness to their Father
—forced, but borne by Him, in conscientious
devotion to them, as willingly as Jesus went
to Golgotha. If at Calvary we find the
rocky coast-line of human thought and feeling opposing the inflow of God, the incoming waters break into the silver spray of
speech, and their one word is Love.

In this revelation of our Father is the

assurance of our forgiveness. Such a God is not one who may or may not be gracious, as He wills; it is "His property always to have mercy." He would not be just in His own eyes, were He unmerciful; He is just to forgive us our sins and to cleanse us from all unrighteousness. Like His Son, He owes us Himself; and His forgiveness is freely ours in the measure that we are able to receive it, that is, in the measure in which we have forgiven others.

Jesus at Calvary proves Himself both our Substitute and our Exemplar. He who finds and opens a trail to a mountain-top encounters and removes obstacles, which none of those who come after him need to meet; he makes the path *for them*. When the sinless Jesus found Himself socially involved with His brethren in the low valley of the world's sinfulness, and looked off to the summit of His Father's perfectness, He felt a separation between the whole world and God; and He gave Himself to end it. We shall never know the uncertainties that shrouded Him and the temptations He faced, from the experience in the wilderness at the outset to the anguish of His spirit in Gethsemane and the consciousness of dereliction on the cross. The "if it be possible" of His prayer suggests the alternative routes He sought to find, before He resigned Himself to opening the path by His blood. Since His death there is "a new and living way" for those who know Him, which stretches from the lowest point of their abasement to the very peak of God's holiness. Up that way they can pass by repentance and trust, and down it the mercy of God hastens to meet and lead them. They are forever delivered from the sense of exclusion from God; the way lies open. But he who knows a path must himself walk it, if he would reach its goal; and no one is profited by Christ's sacrifice who does not give himself in a like sacrificial service; only so does he ever reach fellowship with the Father.

The cross convinces us that we must love one another in the family of God as our Father in Christ has loved us; and it further pledges us God's gift of Himself, that is His Holy Spirit, to fulfil this debt of love. It speaks to us of One who offers nothing less than Himself, and nothing less will do, to be the Conscience of our consciences, the

Heart of our hearts, the Life of our lives. We are lifted by the cross into a great redemptive fellowship, a society of redeemers —the redeeming Father, the redeeming Son and a whole company inspired by the redeeming Spirit. We fill up on our part as individuals and as Christian social groups— churches, nations, families—that which is lacking in the sufferings of Christ for His Kingdom's sake. The more Christian our human society becomes, the more it will manifest the vicarious conscience of its Lord, and feel burdened with the guilt of every wrong-doer, and bound to make its law-courts and prisons, its public opinion and international policies and all its social contacts, redemptive. Through every touch of life with life, in trade, in government, in friendship, in the family, men will feel self-giving love akin to, because fathered by, the love of God commended to the world when Christ died for sinners.

While in a sense men will become all of them redeemers one of another, behind them all will ever lie the unique sacrifice of Jesus. The singularity of that sacrifice lies not in the act but in the Actor: *"He* is the propitiation for our sins; and not for ours only, but also for the whole world." Every member of the redeemed society, however much he may owe to the sacrificial service of his brethren, will feel himself personally indebted to Christ, who loved him and gave Himself up for him. As the Originator of the redemptive fellowship, the Creator of the new conscience, the Captain of our salvation who opened up the way through His death into the holiest of all, we give to Jesus and to no other the title, "The Lamb of God who taketh away the sins of the world."

CHAPTER VI

THE NEW LIFE—INDIVIDUAL AND SOCIAL

The health department of a modern city is charged with a double duty: it has to care for cases of disease, and it has to suggest and enforce laws to keep the city sanitary. The former task—the treatment of sickness—is much more widely recognized as the proper function of the medical profession; the latter —the prevention of the causes of illness—is a newer, but a more far-reaching, undertaking. When Pasteur was carrying on his investigations into the origins of certain diseases, most of the leading physicians and surgeons made light of his work: "How should this chemist, who cannot treat the simplest case of sickness nor perform the most trifling operation, have anything to contribute to medical science?" But Pasteur's discovery of the part played by bacilli not only altered profoundly the work of physicians and surgeons, but opened up the larger task of preventive medicine.

The Gospel of Christ, in its endeavor to make and keep men whole, faces a similarly double labor. It has its ministry of rescue and healing for sinning men and women; it has its plan of spiritual health for society. It comes to every man with its offer of re-birth into newness of life: "If any man be in Christ, he is a new creature." It comes to society with its offer of a regenesis, a para-dise of love on earth. The life of God enters our world by two paths—personally, through individuals whom it recreates, and by whom it remakes society; socially, through a new communal order which re-shapes the men and women who live under it. The New Testament speaks of both entrances of the Spirit of God into human life: it pictures *one* born from above," and "the holy *city* coming down from God out of heaven." The two processes supplement each other. Consecrated man and wife make their home Christian; a Christian home ren-ders the conversion of its children unneces-sary; they know themselves children of God as soon as they know themselves anything at all. Saved souls save society, and a saved society saves souls.

Religion must always be personal; each must respond for himself to his highest inspirations. A child may confuse the divine voice with that of its parents, through whom the divine message comes; but a day arrives when he learns that God speaks directly to him, perhaps differently from the way in which his parents understand His voice, and he must listen for himself alone. A Job may take at second-hand the conventional views of God current in his day, and through them have some touch with the Divine; but this will seem mere hearsay when the stress of life compels him to fight his way past the opinions of his most devout friends to a personal vision of God. Religious experience is hardly worthy the name until one can say, "O God, Thou art *my* God." There is no sphere of life in which a man is so conscious of his isolation as in his dealings with his Highest. The most serious decisions of his life—his apprehension of Truth, his obedience to Right, his response to Love—he must settle for himself.

Space is but narrow—east and west—
There is not room for two abreast.

"Each one of us shall give account of himself to God." In our consciousness of sin, in our penitence, in our faith, others may stimulate and inspire us, may point the way saying, "Behold the Lamb of God," may go with us in a common confession of guilt and a common aspiration towards the Most High, but we are hardly conscious of their fellowship; it is the living God with whom we personally have to do.

> Points have we all of us within our souls
> Where all stand single.

The Gospel comes as a summons to men one by one. Christ knocks at each man's door, offering the most complete personal friendship with him. Were there but a single child of God astray, the Good Shepherd would adventure His life for him, and there is joy in the presence of the angels over *one* sinner that repenteth.

The Evangel has always been good news to sinning people who wished to be different. In *Adam Bede* Mrs. Poyser says of Mr. Craig, "It was a pity he couldna' be hatched o'er again, and hatched different." The Gospel claims to be the power of God which can make the worst and lowest of men—an Iago or a Caliban—into sons of the Most High in the measure of the stature of the fulness of Christ.

This has seemed incredible to most outsiders. Celsus in the Second Century, in his attack on Christianity, wrote, "It must be clear to everybody, I should think, that those who are sinners by nature and training, none could change, not even by punishment —to say nothing of doing it by pity." Dickens' Pecksniff "always said of what was very bad that it was very natural." But it has been the glory of the Gospel that it could speak in the past tense of some at least of the sins of its adherents: "such *were* some of you." Individual regeneration will ever remain a large part of God's work through His Church. Unless we can raise the dead in sin to life in Christ, we have lost the quickening Spirit of God; so long as the world lieth in wickedness, every follower of Jesus must go with Him after men one by one, to seek and to save that which was lost.

But a man's religious experience is vitally affected by social conditions. Moses' protest against the slavery of the Israelites in

Egypt sprang from his feeling that it hindered their fellowship with God. "Let My people go," he felt God saying, *that they may serve Me.*" Mencius, the Chinese sage, wrote: "If the people have not a certain livelihood, they will not have a fixed heart. And if they have not a fixed heart, there is nothing which they will not do in the way of self-abandonment. An intelligent ruler will regulate the livelihood of the people, so as to make sure that, above, they have sufficient wherewith to serve their parents, and, below, sufficient wherewith to support their wives and children; that in good years they shall always be abundantly satisfied, and that in bad years they shall escape the danger of perishing. After this he may urge them, and they will proceed to what is good." Christian workers, today, know well how all but impossible it is to get a man to live as a Christian, until he is given at least the chance to earn a decent living.

But we have to be on our guard lest we overemphasize the force of circumstances either to foster or hamper a man's fellowship with God. The life of Jesus is the irrefutable argument that the Lord's song may be sung in a strange land. It is always possible to be a Christian under the most unfavorable conditions, provided the Christian does not shirk the inevitable cross. But the social order under which men live shapes their characters. Ibsen calls it "the moral watersupply," and religion is intensely interested in the reservoirs whence men draw their ideals.

A glance over a few typical forms of social order will illustrate its influence on character:

Perhaps the noblest society of antiquity was the Greek city state. It expected its citizens to be all of them warriors, statesmen, legislators, judges. It set a premium upon the virtues of courage, self-control, justice and public spirit. It delivered its citizens from that "greasy domesticity" which Byron loathed in the typical Englishman of the Georgian epoch, and made them civic minded. But its ideal was within the attainment of but a fraction of the population. The slaves had no incentive to these virtues; and it is estimated that in Athens in the Fourth Century B. C. there were 400,000 slaves and 100,000 citizens. The many did

the hard work, debarred from the highest
inspirations, in order that the privileged few
might have freedom to achieve their lofty
ideals. And outside the state, or the Greek
world, the rest of mankind were classed as
"barbarians," to whom no Greek ever
thought of carrying his ideals.

Nominally Christian Europe in the
Middle Ages presented in the Feudal System a different type of society. A vast
hierarchy in Church and State, with the pope
and emperor at the top, ran down through
many gradations to the serf at the bottom.
It was an improvement on the little Greek
state in that it embraced many more in a
single order and bound them together with
common faith and standards. It prized not
the civic virtues, but the militarist qualities
of loyalty, obedience, honor, chivalry. Its
typical hero is the Chevalier Bayard, the
good knight without fear and without re-
proach. But a career like his is manifestly
possible only to a few. The agricultural
laborer chained to the soil, and the trader—
often the despised Jew confined to the
Ghetto—had no part in the life of chivalry.
Outside of Christendom the Saracen was to

be converted or slain, and he was far oftener slain than converted.

Under the revival of classical ideals at the Renaissance, in the new emphasis upon individual rights born of the Reformation, in the rebellion of the Puritan English and Scotch against the divine right of kings and bishops to rule them against their conscience and will, in the Revolution of 1789 and the Napoleonic wars, the Feudal System passed, and the commercial order took its place. Its cherished virtues are initiative, industry, push, thrift, independence. As its *beau ideal* it substitutes for the Chevalier Bayard the successful business man. It sincerely tries to open its privileges to everyone; and under favorable circumstances, in Revolutionary America for instance, its ideals were accessible to practically every white inhabitant. The Comte de Ségur, one of the young French officers who came to take part in our War of Independence, wrote: "An observer fresh from our magnificent cities, and the airs of our young men of fashion—who has compared the luxury of our upper classes with the coarse dress of our peasants and the rags of our innumerable

poor,—is surprised on reaching the United
States, by the entire absence of the extremes
both of opulence and of misery. All Ameri-
cans whom we met wore clothes of good
material. Their free and frank and familiar
address, equally removed from uncouth dis-
courtesy and from artificial politeness, be-
tokened men who were proud of their own
rights and respected those of others." But
under other conditions its ethical incentives
are often without appeal to the man who
lacks capital, or to the man with so large
an assured income that he desires no more.
It can do little for the dregs or the froth of
society—those so oppressed that they cannot
rise to its social responsibilities, and those
so lightened that they do not feel them. It
looks upon the so-called backward peoples
as markets where it can secure raw materials
needed for its factories—its rubber, ivory,
jute,—or engage cheap labor, and as a
profitable dumping-ground for its surplus
products. It has done much for the less
developed sections of the race by its missionaries, educators and physicians; but all
their efforts have been almost offset by the
evils of exploiting traders or grasping

government agents, and the exported vices of civilization.

Christianity has a social order of its own—the Kingdom of God. It is not an economic system, nor a plan of government, but a religious ideal—society organized under the love of God revealed in Christ. This ideal it holds up in contrast with the existing social order in any age as a protest, a program and a promise.

The Kingdom *protests* against any features in prevailing conditions that do not disclose Christlike love. It scans the industrial world of today, and finds three fundamental evils in it: competition as a motive, arraying man against man, group against group, nation against nation, in unbrotherly strife; gain-seeking as the stimulus to effort, inducing men to invest capital, or to labor, primarily for the sake of the returns to themselves; and selfish ownership as the reward of success, letting men feel that they can do as they please with their own. Certain callings, upon which the Christian Spirit has exerted a stronger influence, have already been raised above the level of the commercial world. It is not good form professionally

for physicians, or ministers, or college pro-
fessors to compete with each other and seek
to draw away patients, parishioners or
pupils; to exercise their callings mainly for
the sake of financial gains; nor to regard as
their own their skill, or inspiration, or learning. But as yet the butcher, the baker, the
grocer, the banker, the manufacturer, the
promoter, are not supposed to be on this
plane. They are urged to compete, even to
the extent of putting their rivals out of business, in defiance of an old Jewish maxim,
"He that taketh away his neighbor's living
slayeth him," and in face of the Lord's
Prayer in which we ask not for "my daily
cake," but for *our* daily bread." They are
expected to consider profits, dividends,
wages, as the chief end in their callings; and
if out of their gains they devote a portion to
public uses, that is charity on their part. A
few individuals are undoubtedly superior to
the ideal set before them, and are as truly
dedicated servants of the community as any
physician or minister of the gospel, but they
are a small minority; and the false ideal
ruins characters, and renders the commercial

world a battlefield, instead of a household of co-working children of God.

It scans international relations, and finds patriotism still a pagan virtue. Mr. Lecky calls it "in relation to foreigners a spirit of constant and jealous self-assertion." When a tariff is under discussion, high, low or no duties are advocated as beneficial for the industries of one's own country, regardless of the welfare of those of other lands. The scramble for colonies with their advantages to trade, the imperialistic spirit that seizes possessions without respect to the wishes of their inhabitants, the endeavor to secure in other countries special concessions or large business orders at an extraordinary profit, are all sanctified under the name of patriotism. The peace of the world is supposed to be maintained by keeping nations armed to the teeth, so that rival powers will be afraid to fight, and huge armies and navies are labelled insurance against war. A sentence in a letter of Erasmus has a singularly modern sound: "There is a project to have a congress of kings at Cambrai, to enter into mutual engagements to preserve peace with each other and through Europe. But cer-

tain persons, who get nothing by peace and
a great deal by war, throw obstacles in the
way." The armament argument for peace
has been given its *reductio ad absurdum;*
but it is by no means clear that the world-
wide war will free the nations from the
burdensome folly of keeping enormous
armies and navies. As Christians we must
protest without ceasing that international
relations, based on mutual fear and
maintained by the use of brute force, can
never furnish the peace of Christ.

It scans the system of justice in its treatment of the wrong-doer, and declares that
the crude attempt to fit the punishment to
the crime, and to protect society by deterrent
penalties, is not the justice of Him who is
"faithful and just to forgive us our sins and
to cleanse us from all unrighteousness."
Divine justice is redemptive; and society, if
it wishes to be Christian, must pay the heavy
cost of making all its contacts with the im-
perfect transforming.

It scans the educational institutions of
our land, and sees many students viewing
learning only with reference to its immediate
commercial availability, spurning all studies

as "unpractical" which do not supply knowledge that can be coined into financial returns; and it sees many others without intellectual interest, prizing schools and colleges merely for their social pleasures, lazily choosing courses which require a minimum of labor, and disesteeming the great opportunities of culture and enrichment provided by the sacrificial studies and labors of the past. It insists that a moral revival is needed for an intellectual renaissance. All students must be baptized with a passion for social service, before studies that enrich the mind and enlarge the character will be pursued with eager devotion. The blight of irresponsibility is almost universal upon the students in the higher educational institutions of our country.

So the Christian social order contrasts itself with every phase and aspect of our present life, and exposes the impoverishing absence of the Spirit of God. Its protest is reinforced by widespread social restlessness and the feeling that the existing state of things has gone into moral bankruptcy.

But the Kingdom of God is no mere protest; it is a *program* of social redemption.

Some thinkers flatly deny that Christianity
can provide a constructive plan for society.
Mr. Lowes Dickinson makes his imaginary
Chinese official write of the social teachings
of Jesus: "Enunciated centuries ago, by a
mild Oriental enthusiast, unlettered, un-
travelled, inexperienced, they are remark-
able not more for their tender and touching
appeal to brotherly love, than for their aver-
sion or indifference to all other elements of
human excellence. The subject of Augus-
tus and Tiberius lived and died unaware of
the history and destinies of imperial Rome;
the contemporary of Virgil and of Livy
could not read the language in which they
wrote. Provincial by birth, mechanic by
trade, by temperament a poet and a mystic,
he enjoyed in the course of his brief life few
opportunities, and he evinced little inclina-
tion, to become acquainted with the rudi-
ments of the science whose end is the pros-
perity of the state. The production and dis-
tribution of wealth, the disposition of power,
the laws that regulate labor, property, trade,
these were matters as remote from his interests, as they were beyond his comprehension.
Never was man better equipped to inspire a

religious sect; never one worse to found and direct a commonwealth."

Jesus' teaching concerning the Kingdom of God is contained in a handful of parables and picturesque sayings. It attempts no detailed account of a Utopia; it lays down no laws; it offers the world a spirit, which in every age must find a body of its own. But this indefiniteness does not fit it the less, but the better, as the inspiration to social reconstruction. It affords scope for variety and endless progress. It can take up the social ideals of other ages and of other civilizations, and incorporate whatever in them is congruous with the Christian social order. The ideals of Greece and Medieval Europe and of our present commercialism, and the ideals of China, India and Japan, are not to be thrown aside as rubbish, but reshaped and "fulfilled" by Christlike love. It does not stultify human development by establishing a rigid system; but entrusts to thoughtful and conscientious children of God the duty of constantly readjusting social relations, so that they are adequate expressions of their Father's Spirit. In every age Christians are compelled not only to voice their protest against the existing order, but to point out precisely what the Spirit of Christ demands, and try practically to embody it. The fact that our directions are not explicit is proof that God deals with us not as little children but as sons and daughters, not as servants but as friends. We have to think out for ourselves the economic system, the policies of government, the disciplinary methods, the educational ideals, that will incarnate the Spirit of our Father. The all-sufficient answer to the charge of the inadequacy of Jesus as a guide to social welfare is the fact, that only in so far as we are able to express His mind in our social relations, do they satisfy us. The advances made in our generation are conspicuous instances of progress not away from, but up to Him. The crash of our present commercial order in industrial strife, now scarcely heard in the greater confusion of a world at war, gives us the chance to come forward with the principles of Jesus, and ask that they be given a trial in business enterprises that are based on coöperation, the joy of service as the incentive to toil, responsible trusteeship of that which each controls for the benefit of all the rest; in international relations where every nation comes not to be ministered unto but to minister, and loves its neighbors as itself —to ask that we seriously try the social order of love. John Bright, unveiling the statue to Cobden in the Bradford Exchange, said, "We tried to put Holy Writ into an act of Parliament." We want the mind of Christ put into commerce, laws, pleasures and the whole of human life.

And we come forward with confidence, because the Kingdom we advocate is not merely a protest and a program, but also a divine *promise*. The ideal of the Kingdom of heaven to which our consciences respond is for us a religious inspiration, and has behind it a faithful God who would not deceitfully lure us to follow an illusive phantom. "According to His promise we look for new heavens and a new earth wherein dwelleth righteousness." The city of our hope has not been designed by us, but has been already thought out in God's mind and comes down out of heaven. In our attack upon existing injustices and follies we raise again the believing watchword of the Crusaders, *"Deus vult."* In our attempt to rear

the order of love, which cynics pronounce
unpractical, we fortify ourselves in the assurance that it is God's plan for His world,
and that we shall discover a preëstablished
harmony between the Kingdom of heaven
and the earth which we with Him must conform to it. We encourage ourselves by re-
calling that, in the hearts of men everywhere
and in the very fabric and structure of
things, we have countless confederates.

On one of Motley's most glowing pages,
we are told how, after the frightful siege and
fall of Haarlem, and with Alkmaar closely
invested by the Duke of Alva, when the
cause of the Netherlands seemed in direst
straits, Diedrich Sonoy, the lieutenant
governor of North Holland, wrote the
Prince of Orange, inquiring whether he had
arranged some foreign alliance, and received
the reply: "You ask if I have entered into
a firm treaty with any great king or poten-
tate; to which I answer, that before I ever
took up the cause of the oppressed Christians in these provinces, I had entered into a
close alliance with the King of kings; and I
am firmly convinced that all who put their
trust in Him shall be saved by His almighty

hand. The God of armies will raise up armies for us to do battle with our enemies and His own." And the opening of the dykes brought the very sea itself to the assistance of the brave contestants for truth and liberty.

The prayer on our lips, "Thy Kingdom come," we believe to be of God's own inspiring. The social order which we seek is His eternal purpose; and it has sworn confederates in sun and moon and stars of light, and in every human heart. We wait patiently and we work confidently, in the assurance that the God and Father of Jesus Christ, the Lord of heaven and earth, will not fail nor be discouraged, until He has set His loving justice in the earth, and His will is done among all the children of men, as it was once done by His well-beloved Son.

CHAPTER VII

THE CHURCH

No man's spiritual life starts with himself; there is no Melchizedek soul—without father or mother. As our bodies are born of the bodies of others, as our minds are formed from the mental heritage of the race, our faith is the offspring of the faith of others; and we owe a filial debt to the Christian society from which we derive our life with God.

Nor is any man's spiritual experience self-sustaining. Our mental vitality diminishes if we do not keep in touch with thinking people; and brilliant men often lose their lustre for want of intellectual companionship. "Iron sharpeneth iron; so a man sharpeneth the countenance of his friend." A Christian's religious experience requires fellowship for its enrichment, and no large soul was ever grown or maintained in isolation. We are enlarged by sharing the wealthier spiritual life of the whole believing community.

Nor can a religious man contribute his spiritual endowment to the world without joining with kindred souls in an organized effort. Edward Rowland Sill, speaking of his spiritual isolation, wrote to a friend: "For my part I long to 'fall in' with somebody. This picket duty is monotonous. I hanker after a shoulder on this side and the other." The intellectual life of the community organizes itself in schools and colleges, in newspapers and publishing-houses and campaigns of lectures. A learned man may do something by himself for his children or his friends; but he can do incomparably more for a larger public if he is associated with other learned men in a faculty, assisted by the publications of the press, and receives pupils already prepared by other teachers to appreciate his particular contribution. An earnest believer can accomplish something by himself for the immediate circle of lives about him; but he is immeasurably more influential when he invests his inspired personality in the Church, where he finds his efforts for the Kingdom supplemented by the work of countless fellow toilers, where the missionary enterprise bears the impetus of his consecration to thousands he can never see face to face, and where a lasting institution carries on his life-work and conserves its results long after he has passed from earth.

The Christian is dependent upon the Church for his birth, his growth, his usefulness; and this Christian community, or Church, like the intellectual community, instinctively organizes itself to spread its life. There is an unorganized Church, in the sense of the spiritual community, which shares the life of Christ with God and man, as there is an unorganized intellectual community of more or less educated persons who possess the mental acquisitions of the race. But this intellectual community would lose its vitality without its educational agencies; and the spiritual community would all but die were it not for its institutions. The spiritual community is the Church; it is organized in the churches.

As Christians we look back to discover Jesus' conception of the Church. We find it implicit in His life rather than explicit in His teaching. He was born into the Jewish Church which in His day was organized with its Temple and priesthood at Jerusalem, with its Sanhedrin settling its law and doctrine, with its synagogues with their worship and instruction in every town and a ministry of trained scribes, and with a wider missionary undertaking that was spreading the Jewish faith through the Roman world. It was a community with its sectarian divisions of Sadducees, Pharisees and the like, but unified by a common devotion to the one God of Israel and His law. Jesus' personal faith was born of this Church, grew and kept vigorous by continuous contact with it, and sought to work through its organization, for He taught in the synagogues and the Temple.

Jesus does not seem to have been primarily interested either in the constitution, or the worship, or the doctrine of the Jewish Church. He criticised the spirit of its leaders, but did not discuss their official positions. He must have felt that much of the Temple ritual was obsolete, and that many parts of the synagogue services were crude and dull, but He entered into their worship that He might share with fellow believers His expression of trust in His and their God. He did not invent a new theology, but used the old terms to voice His fuller life with God. He was primarily interested in the religious experience that lay back of government, worship and creed; and gave Himself to develop it, apparently trusting a vigorous life with God to find forms of its own. So He never broke formally with the Jewish Church; and even after it had crucified their Master, His disciples are found worshipping in its Temple, keeping its festivals, and observing its law.

But within this Church Jesus had gathered a group about Himself, to whom He imparted His faith and purpose, and into whom He breathed His Spirit. He taught them to think of themselves as salt and light to season and illumine the community about them. As leaders, He bade them become like Himself servants of all. One was their Master, they all were brethren. Soon they developed a corporate feeling that separated them from their fellow Jews, a corporate feeling Jesus had to rebuke because of its exclusiveness: "Master, we saw one casting out demons in Thy name; and we forbade him because he followed not us. But Jesus

said, Forbid him not, for he that is not
against us is for us." On the eve of His
death He kept a Supper with them, which
pictured to them His sustaining fellowship
with them and their comradeship with one
another in Him. And He left them with
the consciousness that they were to carry
forward His work, were possessed of His
inspiring Spirit and had His presence with
them always. Not by Jesus' prescribed
plans, but by His spiritual prompting the
Church came to be. "Like some tall palm
the noiseless fabric sprang."

It was not, then, organization, or ritual, or
creed, that made the Christian Church,
but oneness of purpose with Christ. In the
picture of its earliest days we see it maintaining Jesus' intercourse with God by
prayer; continuing to learn of Him through
those who had been closest to Him; breaking
the bread of fellowship with Him and one
another; expressing that fellowship in a
mutually helpful community life; and all of
its members trying to bear witness to others
of the supreme worth of Jesus. We get at
what they think of themselves by the names
they use: they are "disciples," pupils of the

Divine Teacher; "believers," trusting His
God; "brethren," embodying His spirit
toward each other; "saints," men and women
set apart to the one purpose of forwarding
the Kingdom; "of the Way," with a distinctive mode of life in the unseen and the
seen, following Jesus, *the* Way.   They
called themselves the Ecclesia—the called
out for God's service; the Household of
Faith—insiders in God's family, sharers of
His plans; the Temple of God—those in
whose life with each other and the world
God's Spirit can be seen and felt; the Body
of Christ—the organism alive with His faith
and hope and love, through which He still
works in the earth; the Israel of God, the
holy nation continuing the spiritual life and
mission of God's people of old—no new
Church but the reformed and reborn Church
of God.

The main point for them was that in this
new community the Spirit of God was alive
and at work, producing in its members
Christlike characters and equipping them
for Christlike usefulness.   A body without
life is a corpse; and the Church fairly
throbbed with vitality.   It naturally organ-

ized itself for work, but in organizing it was not conscious of conforming to some fixed plan already laid down, but of allowing the Spirit freely to lead from day to day. Christians found among themselves specially gifted men—apostles (of whom there were many beside the Twelve), with talents for leadership and missionary enterprise—prophets, teachers; and they instinctively held these men highly in love for their works' sake. One thinks of a figure like Paul, who claimed no human appointment or ordination, but whose divine authority was recognized by those who owed their spiritual lives to him. And beside this informal leadership of gifted individuals, a more formal chosen leadership came into existence. God's Spirit used the materials at hand; and Christians in various parts of the Roman world had been accustomed to different types of organization in their respective localities, and these types suggested similar offices in the Church. Some had been accustomed to the town government of a Palestinian village by seven village elders; and this may have suggested "the Seven" chosen in Jerusalem to care for the poor. Some were brought up with the

Oriental idea of succession through the next oldest brother, and this may account for the position of eminence held by James, "the brother of the Lord." Some in Gentile cities had been members of artisan societies, guilds with benefits in case of sickness or death, not unlike lodges among ourselves; and many hints, and perhaps offices (the overseer or bishop, for instance) were taken from them. Some had been familiar with the Roman relationship of patron and client, and when the little groups of converts were gathered together in a wealthier Christian's house, he would be given something of the position of the Roman *patronus*. Still others had been trained in the synagogue, either as Jews or as proselytes, and would naturally follow its organization in their Christian synagogues. There seems to have been variety of form, and along with this variety a felt and expressed unity, with freest intercommunion and hearty coöperation for the evangelization of the world. Throughout there was democracy, so that even a leader so conscious of divine authority as Paul appeals to the rank and file, "I speak as to wise men; judge ye what I say."

In worship, the Church from its early days had the two fixed rites of Baptism and the Lord's Supper; but beside them were most informal meetings for mutual inspiration. "What is it then, brethren: When ye come together, each one hath a psalm, hath a teaching, hath a revelation, hath a tongue, hath an interpretation. Let all things be done unto edifying." Here was room for variety to suit the needs of many temperaments.

And in doctrine there is a similar freedom. One can see in all the Christian speakers and writers in the New Testament an underlying unity in great convictions:—the God and Father of Jesus Christ is their one God; Jesus is their one Lord; they are possessed and controlled by the one Spirit of love; they are confident in a victorious hope; they draw inspiration from the historic facts of Jesus' birth, life, death and resurrection. But they interpret their inspirations in forms that fit in with their mental habits. The fisherman Peter does not think with the mind of the theologically trained Paul, nor does the unspeculative James phrase his beliefs in terms identical with those of the writer to the Hebrews.

Jesus left His Spirit in a group of men; that group gradually was forced out of the national Jewish Church, and became the Church of Christ, dominated by His living Spirit and organizing itself for work, worship and teaching, out of the materials at hand among the peoples where it spread.

We have taken this brief retrospect over the origin of the Church not because it is important for us to discover the precise forms the Church took at the start and reproduce them. It is nowhere hinted in the New Testament that the leaders of these little communities are laying down methods to be followed for all time. Indeed, they had no such thought, for they expected Jesus to return in their lifetime and set up His Kingdom; and they gave scant attention to forms of organization and doctrine that would last but a few years. Nor is it reasonable to suppose that forms which were suited to little groups of people meeting in somebody's house, waiting for their Lord's return, will answer for great bodies of Christians organizing themselves to Christianize the world. No institution can remain changeless in a changing world. "The one immutable factor in institutions," writes Professor Pollard, "is their infinite mutability." Almost all the divisive factors in Christendom are taken out of the past, by those who claim that a certain polity or creed or practice is that authoritatively prescribed for all time, by Christ Himself, or by His Spirit through His personally appointed apostles. The chief question for the Church to decide, when it considers its organization, is—What must we carry on from the past, and what can we profitably leave behind?

The Church of Christ has always been and is one undivided living organism, composed of those who are so vitally joined to Jesus Christ that they share His life with God and men. Our bodies are continually changing in their constituent elements, but remain the same bodies; the spirit of life assimilates and builds into its living structure that which enters the body. The Church of Christ in the world is constantly changing its components as the generations come and go; each new generation is in some respects unlike its predecessor in thought, in usage, in

feeling; but the continuity of the Spirit
maintains the identity of the Body of Christ.
We must carry forward the Spirit of Christ,
and keep unbroken the apostolic succession
of spiritual men and women, all of whom are
divinely appointed priests unto God. We
must realize that, as members in the Body of
Christ, each of us must fulfil some function
for the Kingdom, or we are not living members, but paralyzed or atrophied. There is
a continuity of life in the Church that cannot
be interrupted; we must inherit this life from
the past, and we must pass it on to those who
come after us. Just as the first Christians
felt themselves the Israel of God, so today
we are conscious of being the heirs of patriarchs and prophets, apostles and martyrs,
churchmen and scholars and missionaries,
leaders of spiritual awakenings like Francis
of Assisi, Luther and Wesley, theologians
like Clement, Augustine, Thomas Aquinas,
John Calvin and Jonathan Edwards, and
of countless humble and devoted believers
who have been ruled by the Spirit of the
Master. They have bequeathed to us a
solemn trust; they have enriched us with a
priceless heritage; they have transmitted to

us their life with Christ in God. The
Church comes to us saying:

> I am like a stream that flows,
> Full of the cold springs that arose
> In morning lands, in distant hills;
> And down the plain my channel fills,
> With melting of forgotten snows.

But the historic succession of Christians
through the centuries is not our sole connection with Christ; we not only look *back* to
Him, we also look *up* and look *in* to Him,
for He lives above and in us. The Church is
not a widow, but a bride; and shares its
Lord's life in the world today. The same
Spirit who lived and ruled in the Church of
the first days has been breathed on us,
through the long line of apostolic-spirited
men and women who reach back to Jesus,
and lives and rules in us. We must keep the
unity of the Spirit with the believers of the
past, and with all who are Spirit-led in the
world today; and we must remember that
"where the Spirit of the Lord is, there is
liberty." We are not bound by the prece-
dents of bygone centuries in our organization; we are free to take from the past what
is of worth to us, and we are free to let the

rest go. Is not the Spirit of God as able to take materials at hand in our own age, and to use them for the government, the worship, the creed, the methods of the living Church of Christ?

We cannot, of course, be content with an unrealized unity of the Church. Every little group of Christians, in the first age, felt itself the embodiment in its locality of the whole Church, and it was at one in effort with followers of Jesus everywhere. It exercised hospitality towards every Christian who came within its neighborhood, welcoming him to its fellowship and expecting him to use his gifts in its communion. We want the whole Body of Christ organized, so that it is vividly conscious of its unity, so that it does not waste its energy in maintaining needlessly separate churches, so that followers of Christ feel themselves welcome at every Table of the Lord, and every gifted leader, accredited in any part of the Church, is accepted as accredited in every other where he can be profitably used. The practical problem in Church reorganization is identical with that which confronts society in politics and in industry—how to secure efficient administration while safeguarding liberty, how to combine the solidarity of the group with the full expression of its members' individualities. To be effective the Church must work as a compactly ordered whole. Individuals must surrender personal preferences in order that the Church may have collective force. Teamwork often demands the suppression of individuality. There will have to be sufficient authority lodged in those who exercise oversight to enable them to lead the Christian forces and administer their resources. But we dare not curtail the freedom of conscience, or impede liberty of prophesying, or turn flexibility of organization into rigidity, lest we hamper the Spirit, who divideth to every man severally even as He will. We do not want "metallic beliefs and regimental devotions," but the personal convictions of thinking sons and daughters of the living God, the spontaneous and congenial fellowship of children with their Father in heaven, and methods sufficiently flexible to be adaptable to all needs. We look for an organization of the Church of Christ that shall exclude no one who shares His Spirit, and that shall provide an outlet for every gift the Spirit bestows, that shall bind all followers of Christ together in effort for the one purpose—the Kingdom of God—enabling them to feel their corporate oneness, and that shall give them liberty to think, to worship, to labor, as they are led by the Spirit of God.

Meanwhile there are some immediate personal obligations which rest upon us. We cannot be factors in the organized Church of Christ, save as we are members of one of the existing churches. A Christian should enroll himself either in that communion in which he was born and to which he owes his spiritual vitality, or else in that with which he finds he can work most helpfully. A Christian who is not a Church member is like a citizen who is not a voter—he is shirking his responsibility.

We must free our minds from prejudice against those whose ways of stating their beliefs, whose modes of worship, whose methods of working, differ from our own. We are not to argue with them which of us is nearer the customs of the New Testament; that is not to the point. Wherever we see the Spirit of Christ, there we are to recognize fellow churchmen in the one Church of God. We do not wish uniformity, but variety in unity; for only a Church with a most varied ministry can bring the life of God to the endlessly diverse temperaments of men and women. We are not seeking for the maximum common denominator, and insisting that every communion shall give up all its distinctive doctrines, ritual, customs and activities. We do not want any communion to be "unclothed," but "clothed upon," that what is partial may be swallowed up of fuller life. Dogmatists, be they radicals or conservatives, who insist on a particular interpretation of Christianity, ecclesiastics who arrogantly consider their "orders" superior to those of other servants of Christ as spiritually gifted and as publicly accredited, sectarians so satisfied with the life of their particular segment of the Church that they do not covet a wider enriching fellowship, and churchmen whose conception of the task of the Church is so petty that they fail to feel the imperative necessity of articulating all its forces in one harmoniously functioning organization, are the chief postponers of the effective unity of the Body of Christ.

We have to consider the particular communion to which we ourselves belong, and ask whether there are any barriers in it that exclude from its membership or from its working force those who possess the Spirit of Christ, and so are divinely called into the Church and divinely endowed for service. We must make our own communion as inclusive as we believe the Church to be, or we are not attempting to organize the Church of Christ, but to create some exclusive club or sect of Christians of a particular variety.

We must study sympathetically the ways of other communions, and be prepared to borrow freely from them whatever approves itself as inspiring to Christian character and work. A Presbyterian will often refuse to avail himself of the great historic prayers, simply because he thinks he would be copying Lutherans or Episcopalians, forgetting that he is heir of the whole inheritance of the Church, and that his own direct ecclesiastical forbears freely used a liturgy, and even composed some of the most beautiful parts of the Book of Common Prayer; and an Episcopalian will not cultivate the gift of expressing himself in prayer in words of his own because this is the practice of other communions. As every communion employs in its hymnal the compositions of men and women who in life were members of almost every branch of the Church of Christ, so each should as freely use methods of propaganda, or worship, or education, that have been found valuable in any communion. The more freely we borrow from one another, the more highly we shall prize one another, and the more completely we share the same life, the more quickly will our corporate oneness be felt.

We must set our faces against allowing congregations to embrace but one social class, or several easily combined social strata in the community. In our American towns the Protestant communions are separated more by social caste than by religious conviction. People attend the church where they find "their kind." Poor people do not feel themselves at home, even spiritually, among the well-to-do, and the children of comfortable homes are not permitted to go to the same Sunday School with the children of the tenements. Class lines are as apparent, and almost as divisive, in our churches as anywhere else. The Church of Christ under such circumstances ceases to be a unifying factor in society; its teaching of brotherhood becomes a mockery. In every community there will be found some entirely unchurched social group; and the churches themselves will be impoverished by the absence of the spiritual appreciations to be found most developed in persons of that stratum. Our denominational divisions tend to accentuate our social divisions. Church unity, lessening the number of congregations in a locality, would help to make the churches that remained more socially inclusive. Meanwhile the "one class church," in any but the very rare homogeneous community, ought to realize that, whatever Christian service it may render, it is all the while doing the cause of Christ a great disservice, and is in need of a radical reorganization and an equally radical spiritual renewal into its Lord's wider sympathies.

Personally we must rigidly examine ourselves and test our right to be considered members of the Body of Christ. There are some New Testament evidences of the Spirit that we must still demand of ourselves. One

is loyal obedience to Jesus: "No man can
say, Jesus is Lord, but in the Holy Spirit."
A second is filial trust in God: "Because ye
are sons, God sent forth the Spirit of His
Son into our hearts, crying, Abba, Father."
A third is self-devoting love akin to that
shown on Calvary: "The fruit of the Spirit
is love;" "By this shall all men know that ye
are My disciples, if ye have love one to
another." And if the Spirit is within us, He
is eager to work through us. We may be
quenching Him by laziness, by timidity, by
preoccupation. We are of the Body of
Christ only as we are "members each in his
part."

Above all we must constantly remind ourselves of the Church's adequacy in God for
its work. When we speak of the Church we
are apt to think first of its limitations; when
Paul spoke of the Church its divine resources
were uppermost in his mind—"the Church
which is His Body, the fulness of Him that
filleth all in all." Perhaps the Church's
greatest weakness is unbelief in its own
divine sufficiency. We confront the indifference, the worldliness, the wickedness of
men; we face an earth hideous with war and

hateful with selfishness. We think of the
Church's often absurdly needless divisions,
the backwardness of its thought, the cold-
ness of its devotion, the inefficiency of many
of its methods, the want of consecration in a
host of its members, the imperfections and
limitations of the best and most earnest of
them; and we do not really expect any
marked advance; we hardly anticipate that
the Church will hold its own. Would not
our Lord chide us, "O ye of little faith! all
power is given unto Me in heaven and in
earth, go ye therefore and make disciples of
all nations"? "There are diversities of workings, but the same God who worketh all in
all."

The Church exists to make the world the
Kingdom of God. In the holy city of John's
vision there is no temple, for its whole life is
radiant with the presence of God and of the
Lamb. In the final order there will be no
Church, for its task is finished when God is
all in all. Meanwhile the Church has no
excuse for being except as it continually
renders itself less and less necessary. It has
to lose itself in sacrificial service in order to
save itself. It must never ask itself, "Will

the community support me?" but "Can I inspire the community?" As it seeks to do God's will, it can count on Him for daily bread; a more luxurious diet would not be wholesome for its spiritual life. It exists only to spend and be spent in bringing the children of God everywhere one by one under the sway of His love and presenting them perfect in Christ, and in putting His Spirit in control of homes, industry, amusements, education, government, and the whole life of human society, until we live in "realms where the air we breathe is love."

CHAPTER VIII

THE CHRISTIAN LIFE EVER-
LASTING

Various factors combine to make it hard
for men today to believe vividly in life beyond the grave. Our science has emphasized the closeness of the connection between
our spiritual life and our bodies. If there
be an abnormal pressure upon some part of
the brain, we lose our minds; an operation
upon a man's skull may transform him from
a criminal into a reputable member of society. It is not easy for us to conceive how
life can continue after the body dies. Dide-
rot put the difficulty more than a century
ago: "If you can believe in sight without
eyes, in hearing without ears, in thinking
without a head, if you could love without a
heart, feel without senses, exist when you
are nowhere and be something without ex-
tension, then we might indulge this hope of
a future life."

Our modern view of the universe no longer leaves us a localized heaven and hell, and we have not the lively imaginations of those older generations to whom the unseen world was as real as the streets they walked and the houses in which they lived. One goes into such a burying place as the Campo Santo at Pisa, or reads Dante's *Divina Comedia,* and the painters who adorned the walls with frescoes depicting the future abodes of the blessed and the damned, and the poet who actually travelled in thought through Hell and Purgatory and Paradise, were as keenly aware of these places as of neighboring Italian towns. We lack a definite neighborhood in which to locate the lives that pass from our sight.

Religious authority is based, today, upon experience, and obviously experience can give no certain knowledge of things future. We are disposed to treat all pictures of the life to come, whether in the Bible or out of it, as the projections of men's hopes. They are such stuff as dreams are made on.

And at present we are absorbingly interested in the advance of *our* world's life; we dream of better cities here, rather than of

some golden city beyond our horizon; we
care far more intensely for lasting earth-
wide peace that shall render impossible such
awful orgies of death as this present war,
than for the peace of a land that lieth afar.
Men think of the immortality of their influence, rather than of what they themselves
will be doing five hundred years hence, and
of the social order that shall prevail in the
earth in the year 2000, rather than of the
social order of the celestial country.

Immortality is not so much disbelieved,
as unthought of. But death is always man's
contemporary; and no year goes by for any
of us without regretted partings. And if we
stop to think of it, we are all of us under
sentence, indefinitely reprieved, if you will,
but with no more than an interval between
ourselves and the tomb. To every thoughtful person the question is forced home, "If
a man die, shall he live again?"

What did Jesus Christ contribute towards
answering our question?

He made everlasting life much more
necessary to His followers than to the rest
of men. By bringing life to light and showing us how infinitely rich it is, He kindled in

us the passion for the second life, and rendered immortality indispensable for Christians.

Christ enhances every man's worth in his own eyes. We find that we mean so much to Him and to His God and Father, that we come to mean infinitely more to ourselves. "If," writes a modern essayist, "a man feels that his life is spent in expedients for killing time, he finds it hard to suppose that he can go on forever trying to kill eternity. It is when he thinks on the littleness that makes up his day, on the poor trifles he cares for— his pipe, his dinner, his ease, his gains, his newspaper—that he feels so cramped and cribbed, cabined and confined, that he loses the power of conceiving anything vast or sublime—immortality among the rest. When a man rises in his aims and looks at the weal of the universe, and the harmony of the soul with God, then we feel that extinction would be grievous." And it is just this uplift into a new outlook that men find in Jesus Christ. A Second Century Christian, writing to his friend, Diognetus, characterizes Christianity as "this new interest which has entered into life." We look upon each

day with a fresh expectancy; we view ourselves with a new reverence. The waste
wilderness within, from which we despaired
of producing anything, must under Christ's
recreating touch become an Eden, where we
feel

> Pison and Euphrates roll
> Round the great garden of a kingly soul.

But is this emparadised life to be some
day thrown aside? G. J. Romanes, whose
Christian upbringing had instilled in him the
distinctively Christian appreciation of the
value of his own life, when his scientific
opinions robbed him of the hope of immortality, wrote: "Although from henceforth
the precept 'to work while it is day' will
doubtless but gain an intensified force from
the terribly intensified meaning of the words
that 'the night cometh when no man can
work,' yet when at times I think, as think at
times I must, of the appalling contrast between the hallowed glory of that creed which
once was mine, and the lonely mystery of
existence as I now find it, at such times I
shall ever feel it impossible to avoid the

sharpest pang of which my instinct is susceptible."

And Jesus increases the significance of people for each other. He possessed and conveys the genius for appreciation. He came that life might become more abundant, and every human relation deeper, tenderer, richer. It is to love that death is intolerable. Professor Palmer of Harvard, a few years ago, delivered a lecture upon *Intimations of Immortality in the Sonnets of Shakespere,* in which he showed that, when a man finds himself truly in love, mortality becomes unthinkable to him. And for Christians love and friendship contain more than they do for other men. Christ takes us more completely out of ourselves and wraps us up in those to whom we feel ourselves bound. He makes life touch life at more points, life draw from life more copious inspirations, life cling to life with more affectionate tenacity. He roots and grounds us in love, and that is to root us in the souls of other men; then to tear them from us irrevocably—parents, children, husband, wife, lover, beloved, friend,—is to leave us of all men most pitiable.

> Love—the prisoned God in man—
> Shows his face glorious, shakes his banner free,
> Cries like a captain for eternity.

Again, Christ gives men an ideal for themselves which in their threescore years and ten, more or less, they cannot hope to achieve: "Be ye perfect as your Father." Jesus Himself, in whom we see the Father, is for us that which we feel we must be, yet which we never are. Immortality becomes a necessity to any man who seriously sets himself to become like Jesus. Our mistakes and follies, the false starts we make, the tasks we attempt for which we discover ourselves unfit, the waste of time and energy we cannot repair, the tangled snarls into which we wind ourselves and which require years to straighten out, render this life absurd, if it be final. It cannot be more than a series of tentative beginnings, and if there be no continuation, the scheme of things is a gigantic blunder. If Jesus does no more than supply us with an ideal hopelessly beyond our attainment and inspire us irresistibly to set out on its quest, He is no Saviour but a Tormentor.

The fiend that man harries
Is love of the best.

We are doomed to a few score years of tantalizing failure, and victory is forever impossible for sheer want of time.

Further, Jesus gives men a vision of a new social order—the Kingdom of God—a vision so alluring that, once seen, they cannot but live for its accomplishment. We are fascinated with the prospect of a world where hideous war is unthinkable; where none waste and none want, for brotherhood governs industry and commerce; where nations are animated by a ministering patriotism; and where every contact of life with life is redemptive. But the more fervently we long for this golden age, the more heartily and indignantly we protest against present stupidities and brutalities and injustices, the more passionately we devote ourselves to realize the Kingdom, the more titanic this creation of a new order appears. Nothing we know can remain unaltered; but the smallest improvement takes an unconscionably long while to execute. Haste means folly, and we have to tell ourselves to go

slowly. Things as they are have a fixity
which demands moral dynamite to unsettle.
We ache with curiosity to see how our plans
and purposes will work out; we would give
anything to be in at the finish. But there is
death. We just begin, and then—!

Mr. Huxley, a thorough Christian so far
as his social hope went, though without a
Christian's faith, wrote to John Morley, as
age approached, "The great thing one has
to wish for as time goes on is vigor as long
as one lives, and death as soon as vigor
flags." But the allusion to death set his
mind on a painful train of thought, and he
continued: "It is a curious thing that I find
my dislike to the thought of extinction increasing as I get older and nearer the goal.
It flashes across me at all sorts of times with
a horror that in 1900 I shall probably know
no more of what is going on than I did in
1800. I had sooner be in hell a good deal—
at any rate in one of the upper circles, where
the climate and company are not too trying.
I wonder if you are plagued in this way."
He was repeating the experience of the old
Greeks as it is expressed in Pindar's *Fourth
Pythian:* "Now this, they say, is of all

griefs the sorest, that one knowing good
should of necessity abide without lot therein." It is glorious to hold up before ourselves the splendors of the age that is to be,
to dream of our cities made over in ideals,
of our land as a world-wide servant of righteousness and peace, of a whole earth filled
with truth and beauty and goodwill; and
glorious to give ourselves unremittingly to
bring this consummation nearer. But can
we be content with no personal share in it?
Are our lives merely fertilizer for generations yet unborn?

Oh, dreadful thought, if all our sires and we
Are but foundations of a race to be,—
Stones which one thrusts in earth, and builds thereon
A white delight, a Parian Parthenon,
And thither, long thereafter, youth and maid
Seek with glad brows the alabaster shade,
And in processions' pomp together bent
Still interchange their sweet words innocent,—
Not caring that those mighty columns rest
Each on the ruin of a human breast,—
That to the shrine the victor's chariot rolls
Across the anguish of ten thousand souls!

Tennyson once said to Professor Tyndall
that, if he believed he were here simply to

usher in something higher than himself in which he could have no personal part or lot, he should feel that a liberty had been taken with him. And when that something higher is the Kingdom Jesus proclaimed, its devotees cannot forego their longing to share in its perfected life.

And, above all, Jesus opens up for us an intimacy with God which is both unbearable and incredible without the hope of its continuation beyond the grave. To enter with Jesus into sonship with the Father, to share God's interests and sympathies and purposes, to become the partner of His plans and labors, and then to think of God as living on while we drop out of existence, is the crowning misery, or rather the supreme confusion. Jesus would have pointed to some heartbroken man or woman, like Jairus or the widow of Nain or the sisters at Bethany, and said, "If ye then, being evil, know how to care so intensely for your kindred, and would give your all to keep them with you forever, how much more shall your heavenly Father insist on having His own with Him eternally?"

At Professor Huxley's own request three

lines from a poem by his wife are inscribed upon his tombstone:

> Be not afraid, ye waiting hearts that weep;
> For still He giveth His beloved sleep,
> And if an endless sleep He wills, so best.

But in such a sentence what possible meaning can be put into the expression "His beloved"? Can we conceive of God as really loving us, taking us into His secrets, using us in His purposes, letting us spend and be spent in the fulfilment of His will, and then putting us to an endless sleep? If Jesus leads us into the life with God which we Christians know, He renders immortality indispensable if God is to maintain His own Self-respect.

Others may do without everlasting life; to some an endless sleep may seem welcome; life has been to them such a mistake and a failure, that they would gladly be quit of it forever; but to followers of Jesus its continuance is a passionate and logical longing. Ibsen puts into Brindel's mouth the words: "I am going homewards. I am homesick for the mighty Void; the dark night is best." Jesus acclimatizes man's spirit to a far dif-

ferent home, and sets in his heart an altogether different eternity. So insistent are
the demands of our souls for the persistence
of life with our God in Christ, that "if we
have only hoped in Christ in this life, we are
of all men most pitiable."

Already we have passed into Jesus' second great contribution toward answering
our question of the second life. He assures
us of it because of the character of the Father
we come to know through Him. Jesus' faith
in His own resurrection was based on His
personal experience of God. The words
from a Psalm, which the early Church
applied to Him, sound like an utterance
some disciple may have overheard Him repeating:

Thou wilt not leave My soul in the grave,
Neither wilt Thou suffer Thy devoted One to see cor-
    ruption.
Thou madest known unto Me the ways of life;
Thou shalt make Me full of gladness in Thy presence.

Love is stronger than death, and for Jesus
God is love. It was this which made Him
"the God of the living." Jesus could not
imagine Him linking Himself with men,

becoming the God of Abraham, of Isaac, of Jacob, and allowing them to become mere handfuls of dust in a Hittite grave. His love would hold them in union with Him forever. Jesus "abolished death, and brought life and immortality to light *through the gospel"*—through the good news concerning God. When He succeeds in convincing us that the universe is our Father's house, it requires no further argument to assure us of its "many mansions." The unending fellowship with Jesus' God of all His true children is an inevitable inference from what we know His and our God to be. We do not base our confident anticipation of everlasting life merely upon some saying of Jesus, which we blindly accept because He said it, nor even upon the report of His own resurrection from the grave; these are too slight foundations for our assured expectation. We rest it firmly upon what we know of His and our Father. Immortality is not a mere guess nor a fervent wish; we have solid and substantial experience of what God is from all that He has done for His children and for ourselves. And experience worketh hope. Faith looks both backwards and forwards,

to what God has done and to what He con-
sistently must do; and all the while faith
looks upwards, and in His face reads a love
that will not let us go.

The Easter victory of Jesus is the vindication of His own faith. God, as Lord of
heaven and earth, is involved in our world's
history; He has been responsible for its out-
come from the beginning. If He let the
truest Son He ever had end His career in
defeat and failure, He is a faithless and un-
trustworthy God. Calvary was the supreme
venture of faith; Jesus staked everything on
the responsiveness of the universe to love, in
the trust that the God of the universe is
love. "If Christ hath not been raised, your
faith is vain." But if the seeming triumph
of wrong over right, of ignorance over truth,
of selfishness over sacrifice, which took place
at Golgotha be but the prelude to a vaster
victory, then the Lord of earth has cleared
Himself, and proved Himself worthy of the
confidence of His children.

And of the fact of that victory not only
the first disciples are witnesses, but every
man and woman since in whose life Christ
has been and is a present force. Explain as

we may the details of the resurrection narratives, conceive as we please of the manner in which Christ made Himself known to His followers in His post-resurrection appearances long ago, we know that He is "no dead fact stranded on the shore of the oblivious years," but a living force in our world today, and that Easter triumphs are reënacted wherever His Spirit animates the lives of men. History again and again has demonstrated that His labor has not been vain in God; that the whole structure and fabric of things responds to trust and love; that careers such as His cannot be holden of death, but find an ally in the universe itself, which sends them on through the years conquering and to conquer. That demonstration in history confirms Jesus' trust in God, sets a public seal which the whole world can see to the correctness of His testimony to Him whom He found in the unseen, and in whose cause He laid down His life.

And Jesus has made still another contribution to the answer of our question: it is through Him that we form our pictures of the life to which we look forward so certainly. The New Testament expectations center about Jesus Himself: "With Me in paradise;" "Where I am, there also shall my servant be;" "I go to prepare a place for you;" "So shall we ever be with the Lord." Men who had experienced Christ's hold upon them, through all the divisive circumstances of life, had no doubt of His continuing grasp upon them through death; they spoke of the Christian dead as "the dead in Christ"—the dead under His transforming control. Not death nor life could separate them from His love.

Since we see God, the Lord of heaven, in Jesus, the only and all-satisfying knowledge we have of the future life is that it will accord with the will of the Father of Jesus Christ. Of its details we can merely say, "Eye hath not seen, nor ear heard, neither have entered into the heart of man, the things which God hath prepared for them that love Him." But we know God in Christ: we are certain of many things that cannot be included in a life where His heart has its way; the city of our hope has walls; but it has also gates on all sides and several gates on every side, and we are certain of its hospitability to all that accords with the mind of Christ. That which renders the life within the veil not all dark to us is the fact that "the Lamb is the light thereof." There is a connection between it and our life today; the one Lord rules earth and heaven; and Him we know through Jesus. Humbly acknowledging that we know but in part, glad that the future has in store for us glorious surprises, we are convinced that for us there waits a life in God, in which His children shall attain their Christlike selves in Christlike fellowship one with another and with Him, their Christlike Father. More than this who cares to know? More than this, for what can Christians wish?

Adhæsi testimoniis tuis, Domine.

Psalm. cxviii (119): 31, Vulgate.